Creating your new Kitchen

© Copyright 2003 by PerformaX Publishers

All rights reserved. No part of this book shall be reproduced, stored in a retrieval system, or transmitted by any means – electronic, mechanical, photocopying, recording, or otherwise – without written permission of the publisher.

No liability is assumed with respect to the use of the information contained herein. Although ever precaution has been taken in the preparation of this book, the publisher and authors assume no responsibility for errors or omissions. Neither is any liability assumed for damages resulting from use of the information contained herein.

Traemarks

All terms mentioned in this book that are known to be trademarks or service marks have been appropriately capitalized. PerformaX Publishers can not attest to the accuracy of this information. Use of a term in this book should not be regarded as affecting the validity of any trademark or service mark.

Warning and Disclaimer

Every effort has been made to make this book as complete and accurate as possible but no warranty or fitness is implied. The information provided is on an "as is" basis. The authors and the publisher shall have neither liability nor responsibility to any person or entity with respect to any loss or damages arising from the information contained in this book.

Dedication

We are proud to dedicate *Creating Your New Kitchen* to the hundreds of men and women who have contributed and are contributing, directly and indirectly, to …

- The industry knowledge and skills we apply.
- The broad range of products and services we offer.
- The many customers whose needs we serve.
- The professionals who assist us in meeting those needs.

Most of all, we are indebted to the men and women who staff the showrooms, warehouses and installation crews of Creative Kitchens in Memphis and Collierville TN and in DeSoto County MS. Without them, neither our company nor this book would have been possible.

Denson Ford   Mike Donovan

Collierville TN
July 2003

Preface

Creating Your New Kitchen alternatively might have been called *The Consumer's Guide to Kitchen Development and Remodeling*. Most of the content consists of answers to questions we've been asked by hundreds of customers involved in building new homes or remodeling existing kitchens.

We've organized this information chronologically. That is, it's assembled in order of user need – beginning with basic design considerations and ending with finishing touches for new and remodeled kitchens.

In each subject area, we've attempted to list alternatives and associated cost factors. In addition we've sorted out the positives and negatives that attach to each of the options. As in any construction-related endeavor, there are no perfect designs or materials. Each has attributes and drawbacks. We've tried to identify all of them so that you can make informed decisions and get the most for your kitchen dollar.

We've also provided space for your notes throughout the book. Look at it as a workbook rather than something you'll want to keep forever. Kitchens usually are renovated at about 10-year intervals. A decade from now, change in materials and construction techniques will have made much of the content obsolete. So don't hesitate to use the "Notes" areas on many pages to record your ideas as you go along.

If you're in West Tennessee, North Mississippi or East Arkansas, we'll welcome your visit to Creative Kitchens showrooms at 4646 Poplar Avenue in Memphis, 211 Mt. Pleasant Rd. in Collierville or 3964 Goodman Road in DeSoto County MS. In the alternative, or in addition, you can begin your kitchen planning using software available without charge at www.kitchens-baths.com.

Chuck Tracy, CKD
Senior Design Consultant
Creative Kitchens

Table of Contents

Part I -- The Planning Process   1
   Chapter 1 – Gathering Design Ideas   3
   Chapter 2 – Budgeting   7
   Chapter 3 – Design and Designers   13

Part II – Developing a Plan   17
   Chapter 4 – Planning   21
   Chapter 5 – Measuring the Kitchen   29
   Chapter 6 – Islands   37
   Chapter 7 – Special Needs   39

Part III – Cabinetry   41
   Chapter 8 – Selecting Cabinetry   43
   Chapter 9 – Types of Kitchens   47
   Chapter 10 – Cabinet Construction   51
   Chapter 11 – Doors and Drawers   53
   Chapter 12 – Accessories   57
   Chapter 13 – Space-Saving Ideas   59
   Chapter 14 – Hardware   61

Part IV – Other Products and Materials   63
   Chapter 15 – Countertops   65
   Chapter 16 – Appliances   69
   Chapter 17 – Sinks and Faucets   79
   Chapter 18 – Flooring   83
   Chapter 19 – Lighting   87
   Chapter 20 – Architectural Detail   91
   Chapter 21 – Walls and Ceilings   93
   Chapter 22 – Windows and Doors   97
   Chapter 23 – Molding and Trim   99
   Chapter 24 – One-of-a-Kind Items   101

Part V – The Construction Process   103
   Chapter 25 – Scheduling   105
   Chapter 26 – Potential Installation Problems   109

Chapter 27 – Survival	111
Chapter 28 – Communication	113
Chapter 29 – Helpful Tips	115
Chapter 30 – Record-Keeping	125

Part I
The Planning Process

Plan the work. Then, work the plan. It's timeworn advice but a very practical way to accomplish complex tasks.

Unfortunately, it's also a path that's more talked about than used, especially in planning kitchens -- new or renewed. The reason is simple: the process appears straightforward and uncomplicated. In one sense, it is. In another, it isn't.

Everyone is familiar with the several components that must come together in a kitchen. Unfortunately, familiarity *does* breed contempt. "I'm familiar with it; therefore, it must be easy" is the unwritten assumption.

It's a poor assumption. Yes, everyone is familiar with the components individually. But few know just how to make them come together successfully. There are too many variables – too many cabinet designs, too many kinds of material, too many styles and too many finishes. And the same range of choices exists in countertops, appliances, sinks and faucets, flooring, architectural detail, lighting and wall finishes.

Without a comprehensive plan, problems are all-but-inevitable. And those problems can be expensive!

The complexities, the problem potential and the associated costs are the reasons for this book. It encompasses knowledge gained by the authors in almost a half century of kitchen construction and modernization – knowledge that will be as helpful to those planning new homes as those preparing to renovate kitchens.

How can this be the case? Because many who build new homes neglect the fact that the typical kitchen is replaced in little more than 10 years, and that decisions made when the home is built create limitations for the future.

Creating Your New Kitchen

How should you proceed? By following a natural progression that begins with gathering ideas and ends in selecting wall finishes and flooring. The steps:

- Gathering ideas
- Establishing a budget
- Weighing product and material options
- Choosing appliances
- Selecting cabinets
- Deciding on countertops
- Picking sinks and faucets
- Choosing architectural detail
- Deciding on wall finishes
- Selecting flooring
- Creating the kitchen

Let's begin!

Notes

Chapter 1
Gathering Design Ideas

We live in the age of information, which can be a blessing or a curse. The volume of information available to those planning new homes or kitchen renovations is tremendous. Among sources worthy of attention:

- Local libraries

- Traditional and online book stores

- A myriad of "home and garden" publications

- Specialized "how to do it" books and planning guides

- Retailers dealing in kitchen components

- Manufacturers and distributors of kitchen components

Where should you begin? At the risk of appearing to over-simplify, your greatest need will be a filing system. You'll find it all-too-easy to fill a file drawer with everything from photos torn from magazines to manufacturers' brochures. The filing system can consist of a set of manila folders or a so-called "expansion" file with multiple pockets. Both are available at any office supply store.

You may want to simply file ideas at the outset, but you'll also want to gather and organize price information and cost estimates as you go along. A folder will be sufficient when you begin but you'll later want to consider storing this information in your computer – preferably in an Excel file designed to make comparisons easy.

Label the files and you're ready to begin. Logical categories:

- Design ideas

- Budgeting

4   Creating Your New Kitchen

- Cabinets
- Appliances
- Countertops
- Flooring
- Sinks and faucets
- Architectural detail
- Wall coverings

Begin at the beginning. You may find it convenient to pick up a great deal of specific information early on, but much of it will prove to be useless before you've finished for one reason: it's impractical to select cabinets, appliances, materials and the like before you've decided on kitchen style and basic configuration. When the basics have been established, in contrast, you'll be able to limit your component and material choices to those items that complement or fit well with your overall plan.

Where you begin is another matter. You can start gathering information at any of the locations identified above. But logic suggests that some are more appropriate than others. It all depends on your tastes and preferences.

If you simply have to have the "in" thing, there's no substitute for periodicals – the many magazines dedicated to homes, gardens and the like. They exist to keep readers abreast of the latest trends, and they do a good job of it. But the trends on which they report can change with mercurial speed.

Books often provide more – but necessarily less current – information. They take longer to move through the publishing process. Most "home" magazines publish at monthly intervals. The typical book can be 12 to 18 months in preparation. That's a lifetime for the style-conscious.

Books in local libraries may or may not be current. Look at the copyright dates shown on introductory pages. Books copyrighted during the past or current years are of recent vintage. Anything older is open to question.

The same guidelines apply in looking at book merchants' online sites. But some of those sites nevertheless can be used to your advantage. The best of them – from a content standpoint – is amazon.com. In addition to a picture of the book's cover, amazon.com usually provides:

- A number of pages from the book
- A table of contents
- Reader reviews
- Perhaps the largest selection on the Internet.
- An excellent search engine permitting you to search and sort by subject and year of publication as well as by author and title.

Literature published by manufacturers of cabinetry, appliances, and accessories often is most current. You should recognize, however, that manufacturers' lines change in keeping with design trends. Some models are discontinued. Others are introduced. Designers associated with kitchen and bath specialty stores can tell you which are newest [or oldest] among those shown in current brochures. The new are likely to be around for several years. The old may not survive the next 12 months.

World Wide Web sites may or may not be good sources of information. Some are regularly revised and contain pictures of everything a manufacturer or distributor has to offer. Others are less

6 Creating Your New Kitchen

current and less reliable. Unfortunately, the visitor seldom can tell the difference.

Need really reliable information fast? Consider visiting a kitchen renovation specialist – a firm that sells and installs cabinets and other kitchen essentials. These organizations almost always will have detailed and accurate technical information supplied by manufacturers on multiple lines of cabinets, appliances, accessories and other project components. Most stay abreast of design trends and some employ design professionals who can assist you with your project. Retainer fees occasionally are charged but these usually are credited against your purchases.

You'll be dealing with a mass of information, but there's one way to keep the process manageable: limit your search by setting a budget, selecting a basic style, and establishing other limiting criteria before you begin.

Notes

Chapter 2
Budgeting

Three major elements are involved in each and every construction project – big or small: quality, price and speed. The buyer can select any two! One must be sacrificed to gain the others, or concessions must be made on all three.

Other governing criteria:

- Your tastes [some styles are more expensive than others]

- Your budget [how much you want to spend]

- Overall project size and complexity

- Degree of change in structural components such as walls [for those planning to renovate a kitchen]

Let's deal with the last element first. Remember our earlier comment about the [approximate] 10-to-15-year renovation cycle for kitchens? About thinking ahead whether planning a new home or renovating? Here's why:

Moving or rearranging water lines, in-slab ventilation lines, and electrical circuits will add large sums to any renovation project. And your preferences can lead you in that direction when renovating an older kitchen.

Want an island [they're relatively new in kitchen design]? If your kitchen is on a slab, you can still have your island, but adding a sink or cook-top can add substantially to your cost. Electrical and/or water lines have to be extended through the concrete.

Some building codes require electrical outlets in islands but these provisions often can be avoided by making islands movable. This is accomplished by adding heavy-duty casters hidden behind a molding that extends to within a quarter inch of the floor. The island appears stationery but isn't.

The cost of major features is much lower in original construction. You don't have to tear out the old before starting to build the new. But that doesn't mean you can afford everything you'd like to have. You're going to have to make choices – a lot of choices – before you begin.

You'll find them easier to make if you focus on exactly what you're trying to achieve. Do you want to:

- 'Spruce up' your home to make it more saleable?

- Make a few improvements to serve until the teenagers leave home?

- Create the perfect kitchen to use for a long time?

Knowing what you want will help you decide what to buy and how much you want to spend. Your buying decisions should be based on personal preferences if you're "in for the long haul" or on market "preferences" if you're planning on selling.

"The experts" tell us that a kitchen represents 10 to 20 percent of the value of a home. If your home should sell for $250,000, your kitchen budget then should fall in the $25,000 to $50,000 range. Spend too little and the kitchen won't meet buyer expectations. Spend too much and you'll lose money when you sell.

Market preferences are not that difficult to pinpoint. Ask a designer at a kitchen and bath store what features are being chosen most often for new kitchens and/or renovation projects. Then, try to incorporate as many of them as possible in the kitchen you're dressing up for resale. Quiz the designer on features and accessories that will generate the most appeal for the fewest dollars.

Deciding on what to buy is relatively easy when you're planning on selling. The decision-making gets more difficult when you're going to stay and use the kitchen yourself. You'll find the process easier if you'll:

- Sort out kitchen features into three categories: must have, could do without, and unimportant.

- Set a budget target – the number of dollars you can afford to spend.

- Obtain prices on all the components of your "perfect" kitchen.

You're among the favored few if the cost of your perfect kitchen falls within your budget. If it doesn't, you'll have to start looking for ways to reduce the total. Some methods you might consider:

- Downgrading materials in one or more areas.

- Eliminating one or more "pricey" features.

- Working with your builder's or your cabinet company designer instead of one of your community's "big names."

The basics are the same in every kitchen:

- Cabinetry

- Appliances

- Countertops

- Sinks and faucets

- Flooring

- Wall finishes

- Moldings and other architectural details

And each can be "downgraded" a bit to save some money. You might, for example, consider using:

- Maple instead of cherry in your cabinets.
- Free-standing rather than built-in appliances.
- Patterned laminate with special edge treatments rather than granite or solid surface countertops.
- Vinyl or wood instead of stone flooring.
- Undermounted instead of integral sinks.
- Designer-styled faucets without ceramic lifetime cartridges.
- Vinyl-covered rigid foam rather than hardwood moldings.
- Sponge-painted instead of stucco walls.

In most areas, you'll find inexpensive, moderately-priced and luxury products from which to choose. The choices are very personal. You'll often be able to "go first class" in one area by scaling down in others.

In the appliance area, for example, most agree that every kitchen needs a range, oven, refrigerator, dishwasher and disposal. Do you also need a trash compactor, a microwave, a warming drawer, a wine chiller, a hot water dispenser, a built-in icemaker, a television and a radio?

Similarly, you must have cabinets, but do you need a spice rack, a built-in wine rack, an appliance garage, a breadbox, cutlery and recycling storage areas, divided drawers, adjustable shelves, lazy susans and glass door fronts?

You'll also want to deal carefully with two other variables through which costs can be contained or permitted to run amuck. One is the interest you'll pay if you're financing a renovation project or a new home. Negotiating with lenders can result in lower interest rates and significant savings.

The second is design. Potential savings exist in your selection of a basic design scheme for your kitchen and in your decisions concerning the team you put together to make the kitchen a reality. We'll discuss both in the next chapter.

But what should it all cost? You probably can do a facelift – including laminate counter tops and cabinet refinishing – for less than $15,000. The typical major remodeling usually costs $20,000 to $50,000. A cost-is-no-object project can exceed $150,000. What should you expect in each category?

The facelift usually involves:

- Leaving existing cabinets in place but painting or refacing them and replacing hardware.

- Replacing only those appliances that demand replacement with standard, free-standing models.

- Limiting yourself to cast iron or stainless steel sinks.

- Floating a new vinyl floor over your old one.

- Perhaps adding a ceramic tile backsplash.

The mid-range remodeling may include:

- Installing semi-custom or custom cabinetry.

- Using solid-surface countertops, perhaps with natural stone on an island.

- Built-in appliances with panels to match the cabinetry.
- Using an undermount or integral sink.
- Hardwood or ceramic tile flooring.

Upscale remodeling may involve:

- Custom cabinets with unique finishes and/or door styles.
- Stone or solid-surface countertops.
- Commercial-style appliances or those with high performance features.
- An oversize refrigerator and a second dishwasher and sink.
- A vaulted ceiling with skylights, French doors or a bay window.

Notes

Chapter 3
Design and Designers

Design and designers can be inexpensive or costly. If you've a French country home and you've got to have a matching kitchen created by an interior decorator, get ready to spend. If the home is of contemporary design and the kitchen need follow no period motif, you may be able to decorate yourself and save a considerable sum.

Level of complexity and risk of problems also require attention. The more complex the task, the greater the possibility that problems will arise and that you'll have to deal with costly solutions. Designers are paid to apply their knowledge and experience to minimize the risks and avoid the problems. Ultimately, you'll have to decide how you want to proceed.

One design firm has identified 17 distinct home styles that presumably can be extended from exterior design through the interior of every room – including the kitchen – if you can afford it. You're going to pay substantial premiums in at least two ways.

First, you'll be faced with additional expense to ensure that every component of the kitchen conforms to the specified style. Cabinetry usually accounts for 50 to 60 percent of the cost of a kitchen, and no manufacturer offers cabinets in every style. You may well find yourself confronted with higher prices to maintain the décor you prefer.

Second, you may pay a premium – in one way or another – when it's time to sell the home. Relatively few prospective buyers are likely to be enamored of your favorite style. As a result, you may have to compromise on your sale price or wait a long time for the right buyer to come along.

You'll encounter similar pitfalls in other areas as well. Your color scheme, for example, may or may not appeal to prospective purchasers. That's why the interiors of most homes built "for the market" are painted in what's come to be known as "builder's beige" –

a pale tan with a bit of gray mixed in – that will compliment or, at minimum, will not clash – with just about any furnishings a prospective buyer might own.

If you do a bit of investigating, you'll also find that the use of color changes from year to year – that some are "in" and others are "out" regardless of any individual's tastes. The Color Marketing Group and the Pantone Color Institute publish annual "palettes" of "in" colors for decorators and others. The new may appear to differ little from the old but they do change. If they didn't, there would be little reason for the Color Marketing Group or the Pantone Color Institute to exist.

You'll want the services of a designer to help avoid downstream problems. The challenge you and he or she will face is simultaneously simple and complex. You need a design and a color scheme that meet your requirements without going so far as to be offensive to others – especially those who one day may be interested in buying your home.

The designer you select can be an architect or a member of an interior design firm. Each will charge fees ranging from the hundreds to the thousands of dollars depending on the extent of the services you require. Design services also are available at nominal cost and may be provided without cost by your cabinet supplier.

The "gold standard" in kitchen design is the Certified Kitchen Designer [CKD] designation of the National Kitchen and Bath Association. Some certified designers operate their own firms or work for interior decorators. Others are employed by kitchen renovators and cabinet suppliers.

One of the earliest – and most important – decisions you'll have to make is the nature of your development team. It you're remodeling or restoring an older home or building a new one, you'll rely primarily on a general contractor who will hire and supervise subcontractors as necessary. Design guidance may be available through the contractor but more often will be provided by an independent architect or interior designers – at your expense, of course.

Creating Your New Kitchen 15

At the opposite end of the spectrum is a "single source provider" – usually a kitchen and bath cabinetry and remodeling firm – which will contract with you to provide a "turn key" job. That firm will provide everything you need from design, plans and specifications to final inspection. You'll deal with a designer who also may serve as project manager, coordinating the many suppliers whose products and services go into the finished kitchen.

What's the difference? Assuming comparable outcomes, you'll probably save with the single source provider for one reason: there will be less vendor profit involved. Look at it this way, if you hire an architect, an interior design firm, and a contractor, each will assign personnel to the project. Owners' profits will be added to all of their wages. The single source provider, in contrast, has but one profit.

The dollar savings involved may be substantial or nominal. The time savings, will be tremendous. And the reduction in the "hassle factor" will be priceless. You'll deal with only one firm – usually with only one individual within that firm – rather than with multiple vendors, each of them all too ready to blame the others for any problems that might arise.

Whatever course you take, guard yourself in the clinches. The Better Business Bureau recommends you follow these steps:

- Plan your project carefully.

- Explain exactly what you want to all contractors. Better yet, put it in writing.

- Approve any plans before work begins, and don't let work begin without your approval of a complete set of plans.

- Compare costs before entering into contracts. Obtain bids or proposal, and make certain they are comparable.

- Obtain references and check them.

- Contact your Better Business Bureau and check on prospective vendors before you signing contracts.

- Make certain your vendors are insured against claims for worker compensation, property damage and personal liability.

- Contact state, county or city housing authorities to be certain your contractor meets all licensing and bonding requirements.

Should changes of any kind be made in the project after work begins, make certain you have a clear understanding of any differences in cost that may be involved, and get them in writing.

Other things to consider before you begin: your lifestyle and its implications, time as well as economic variables, and matters of style.

Consider the basics. Are you satisfied with the size, traffic flow and storage capacity if your existing kitchen? What changes do you want to make?

Will your kitchen be limited to cooking or will it become a central gathering place for family and guests?

What kind of appearance do you want for the kitchen and environs?

What sort of schedule does the project require? Are there holidays or vacations to be avoided? Weather considerations if you're going to change exterior walls?

What does the neighborhood imply as to finished costs? You don't want to invest so much in a new kitchen that you've "priced yourself out of the market" when it comes time to sell.

Part II
Developing a Plan

Plan your work; work your plan. And you'll accomplish your objectives and reach your goal.

Creating a kitchen is a complex task. Replacing an old kitchen with a new one is even more complicated. Pause for a moment and think about the knowledge and skills required. In one form or another, you're going to need:

- A set of construction plans, which usually have to be stamped by an architect and/or an engineer.

- A design, which you may be able to do yourself but may be better left to a professional designer.

- Workers to rip out the old kitchen if you're going to be remodeling.

- Carpenters to build any new walls or wall/ceiling segments that may be necessary.

- Plumbers to remove old plumbing and/or install new.

- Electricians to remove old wiring and/or install new.

- Installers for ...
    - Cabinetry
    - Millwork
    - Countertops
    - Lighting fixtures
    - Appliances
    - Flooring
    - Wall coverings

- Inspectors or supervisors to make certain the work is done properly.

18   Creating Your New Kitchen

If you're building a new home, your general contractor will assume responsibility for seeing that your wishes are carried out. Renovation projects are another matter. By their nature, they require even closer supervision and tighter control. You can handle these tasks yourself or assign them to others, but they've got to be done.

Remember, what's everyone's responsibility is no one's responsibility. And trying to resolve problems where all involved deny fault is costly in time, money and ulcers.

As you read about the planning process in the following pages, you'd do well to consider carefully whether you really want to be your own general contractor and, if not, how you want your renovation project managed. And keep the design basics – layout, storage, counter space and lighting – in mind.

Layout – Don't hesitate to change the shape of the kitchen to improve work flows if space permits.

- A U-shaped kitchen surrounds the cook with the work, but requires an additional sink to accommodate more than one cook.

- L-shaped kitchens offer two continuous runs of counter space and can be especially attractive if floor space permits an island.

- Galley-style kitchens keep appliances close at hand but traffic can disrupt cooking.

- One-wall kitchens require long back-and-forth trips from on area to another.

Storage – Begin with a careful evaluation of existing storage and display features. Then think about:

- Adding exposed storage.

- Placing items where they are first or last used, such as large pots near the sink.

- Storing seldom-used items outside the kitchen to free up cabinet space.

- Allowing for expansion space, perhaps in the form of an oversized dinette to which cabinets can be added later.

Counter space – You can't have too much. The National Kitchen & Bath Association recommends 11 square feet at least 16 inches deep for small kitchens, at least 16.5 feet for larger kitchens. Other considerations:

- Cooking surfaces should have at least 12 inches of counter space on either side. Additional space should be provided for microwave ovens and refrigerators.

- A landing area for in-coming groceries.

- Designated areas for small appliances – toasters, coffeemakers, food processors and the like – perhaps in appliance garages positioned in deep corners.

Lighting – Kitchens require three types of lighting: task, general, and accent.

- Light worker areas rather than floor space with special attention to the sink, range and the fronts of counter tops.

- Make certain you'll not cast shadows over work areas.

- Use under-cabinet lighting above counters, with baffles to keep the light from shining into your eyes when you're seated.

Notes

Chapter 4
Planning

Whether you're preparing to build a new home or renovate an older kitchen, you need a plan.

"But won't I just use the existing kitchen space?"

Perhaps; perhaps not. More often than not, those who renovate kitchens make significant changes by capturing nearby spaces – dinettes, laundry rooms, pantries, mud rooms etc. – or by otherwise changing basic kitchen configurations.

The objective in every case is a bigger kitchen, a better kitchen, a more functional kitchen, a more attractive kitchen, or all of the above. In most cases, the homeowner wants at least two or more of these advantages. They can be obtained in any of a number of ways, but the most convenient among them involves creating a plan that meets the guidelines of the National Kitchen and Bath Association.

The guidelines may be more detailed than you need them to be, but each and every one is worthy of consideration. They were created to ensure that your kitchen design will:

- Limit walking distances between major work places.
- Provide sufficient space for all functions.
- Have adequate storage areas.
- Accommodate two or more cooks simultaneously.
- Easily rinse dishes and load a dishwasher.
- Provide for a range or a separate cooktop and oven.
- Allow for two sinks.

- Accommodate an eating area.

Traffic and Workflow Requirements

- Doorways at least 32 inches wide and not more than 24 inches deep in direction of travel.

- Walkways at least 36 inches wide.

- Work aisles at least 41 inches wide for one cook; 48 inches wide for two or more cooks.

- Work triangles totaling 26 feet or less with no leg shorter than four feet or longer than nine feet.

- No major traffic patterns crossing through the work triangle.

- No entry, appliances or cabinet doors interfering with one another.

- In seating areas, 36 inches of clearance from counter or table edge to wall or obstruction if no traffic passes behind diners; 65 inches of clearance for walkway behind seated diners.

Cabinets and Storage

- Kitchens smaller than 150 square feet: 144 inches of wall cabinet frontage with cabinets at least 12 inches deep and 30 inches high with adjustable shelving.

- Kitchens larger than 150 square feet: 186 inches of wall cabinet frontage with cabinets at least 12 inches deep and 30 inches high with adjustable shelving.

- At least 60 inches of wall cabinet frontage within 72 inches of primary sink's centerline.

Creating Your New Kitchen 23

- Kitchens of less than 150 sq. ft.: 156 inches of base cabinet frontage with cabinets at least 21 inches deep
Kitchens larger than 150 sq. ft.: 192 inches of base cabinet frontage with cabinets at least 21 inches deep.
Kitchens smaller than 150 sq. ft.: at least 120 inches of drawer or rollout shelf frontage.
Kitchens larger than 150 sq. ft.: at least 165 inches of drawer or rollout shelf frontage.

- At least five storage/organizing items 15 inches to 48 inches above finished floor.

- At least one corner storage unit.

- At least two waste receptacles: one for garbage and one for recyclables.

Appliance Placement and Use

- Knee space below or adjacent to sinks, cooktops, ranges, and ovens at a minimum of 27 inches high by 30 inches wide by 19 inches deep.

- Clear floor space of 30 inches x 48 inches at sink, dishwasher, cooktop, oven, and refrigerator.

- Minimum of 21 inches clear floor space between edge of dishwasher and any object placed at right angle to dishwasher.

- Edge of primary dishwasher within 36 inches of one sink edge.

- Primary sink between or across from cooking surface preparation area or refrigerator.

- At least 24 inches of clearance between cooking surface and protected surface above or 30 inches of clearance between cooking surface and unprotected surface above.

- Ventilation system with a fan rated at a minimum of 150 cubic feet per minute for major surface cooking appliances.

- No cooking surface below operable window unless window 3 inches or more behind appliance and more than 24 inches above it.

- Bottom of microwave ovens 24 to 48 inches above floor.

Counter surface and landing space

- At least two work counter heights: one at 28 inches to 36 inches above finished floor and one at 36 inches to 45 inches above finished floor.

- Kitchens under 150 sq. ft.: at least 132 inches of usable counter frontage. Kitchens over 150 sq. ft.: at least 198 inches of usable counter frontage.

- At least 24 inches of counter frontage to one side of primary sink and 18 inches on other with 24 inches space at same height as sink.

- At least 3 inches of counter frontage on one side of secondary sink and 18 inches on other with 18 inches of space at same height as sink.

- At least 15 inches of landing space (minimum 16 inches deep) above, below, or adjacent to microwave oven.

- Open-ended kitchen: at least 9 inches of counter space on one side of cooking surface and 15 inches on other, at same height as appliance. Enclosed kitchen: at least 3 inches of clearance space at an end wall protected by flame retardant material and 15 inches on other side at same counter height as appliance.

Creating Your New Kitchen 25

- At least 15 inches of counter space on latch side of refrigerator or on either side of a side-by-side or at least 15 inches of counter space no more than 48 inches across from refrigerator.

- At least 15 inches of landing space (minimum 16 inches deep) next to or above oven if it opens into primary traffic pattern; if it does not open into traffic, 15 inches x 16 inches landing space needed.

- Continuous countertop 36 inches long and at least 16 inches deep for preparation center; prep center located by water source.

- For two adjacent work centers, a minimum counter frontage equal to the longest of the two required counter lengths plus 12 inches.

- No two primary work centers separated by full-height, full-depth tall tower unit (i.e. pantry or refrigerator).

- Minimum clearances for seating areas:
    o 30-inch high table/counter: 30 inches wide x 19 inches deep table/counter for each seated diner with 19 inches of clear knee space
    o 36-inch high counter: 24 inches wide x 15 inches deep counter space for each seated diner with 15 inches of clear knee space
    o 42-inch high counter: 24 inches wide x 12 inches deep counter space for each seated diner with 12 inches of clear knee space
    o No sharp counter edges

Room, Appliance and Equipment Controls

- Controls, handles, and door and drawer pulls operational with one hand.

26 *Creating Your New Kitchen*

- Wall-mounted room controls 15 inches to 48 inches above finished floor.

- Ground fault circuit interrupters specified on all outlets.

- Fire extinguisher visibly located in kitchen away from cooking gear and 15 inches to 48 inches above floor.

- Window/skylight area covering at least 10 percent of total square footage of kitchen or total living space that includes kitchen.

- Every work surface well-illuminated by appropriate task and/or general lighting.

A few basic guidelines for planning purposes:

- Keep the work triangle between 13 and 23 feet.

- Place food storage [refrigerator, etc.] near the preparation area.

- Provide adequate task and background lighting.

- Remember that appliances require 24-inch counter tops.

- At minimum, provide a double-bowl sink [one bowl with garbage disposer].

- Provide at least one double electrical outlet for each working area.

- Use swing-out racks in corner cabinets for easy access.

- Place sink, dishwasher, ice-maker and other water-using appliances near a water line to minimize plumbing costs.

- Provide deep drawers under cooktop for pots and pans.

- Provide counter space beside ovens.

- Group tall storage units, oven units, etc., rather than letting them interrupt work surfaces.

Notes

Notes

Chapter 5
Measuring the Kitchen

When you've decided what you want and what will fit, it's time to start measuring the available space. Every designer you encounter is going to want to know what he or she is going to have to work with. Yes, the individual you select will come out to measure and offer specific suggestions, but many of those you'll encounter in gathering information will need dimensions just to provide cost estimates on specific products and services. Here's how NKBA suggests you obtain them.

Note: Don't include current cabinetry or other furniture that won't be kept, and keep all your measurements in inches [don't convert to feet and inches].

Sample Drawing

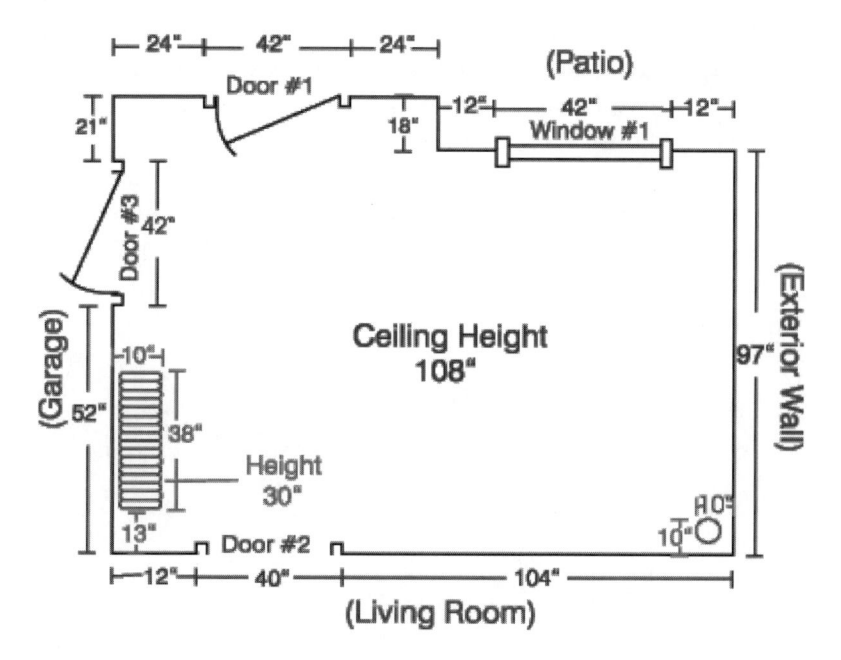

STEP 1
Draw a rough outline of your kitchen. Use the following symbols in your drawing for doors and windows.

30 *Creating Your New Kitchen*

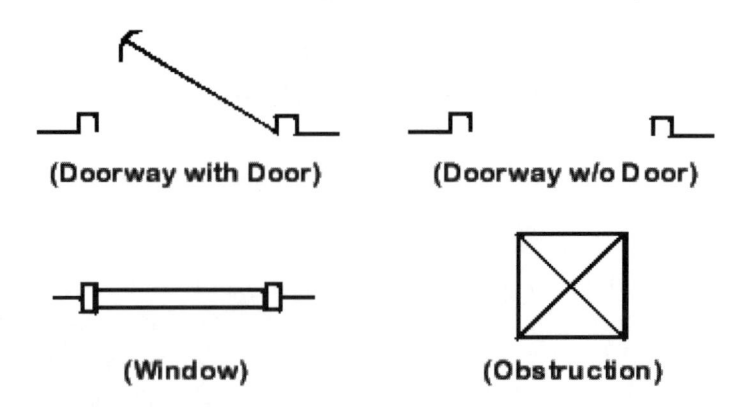

(Doorway with Door)   (Doorway w/o Door)

(Window)   (Obstruction)

NOTE: For doorways with doors, draw the doorway according to which way the door swings.

STEP 2
Draw in any obstructions, such as radiators, pipes, sink plumbing, etc., that you either cannot move or do not want to move.

STEP 3
A) Beginning at the top left corner of your drawing measure to the first window, door, or wall. Continue clockwise around the room until each wall, window and door has been measured.

Note: When measuring doors and windows the trim is considered part of the door or window. As shown in the drawing below, measure from the outside of the trim on one side to the outside of the trim on the other side.

Creating Your New Kitchen 31

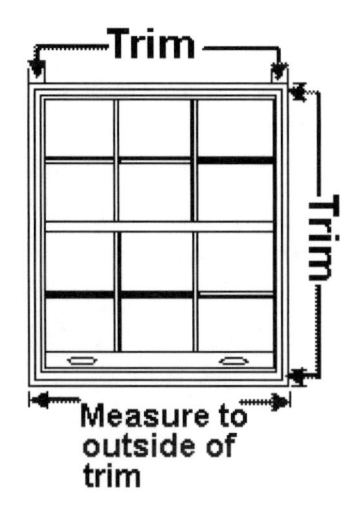

B) Measure the ceiling height and write it in the center of your drawing. Sometimes, especially with older homes, it is a good idea to take measurements in a few different areas of the kitchen. Ceiling heights, even in the same room, can sometimes vary by as much as a few inches.

C) As shown in the drawing below, measure from the floor to the bottom of each window and also measure the overall window height. If you have printed these instructions, write the measurements in the table provided below.

32 *Creating Your New Kitchen*

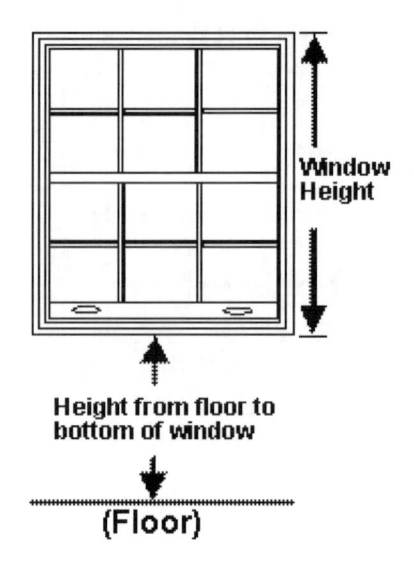

Window Height

Height from floor to bottom of window

(Floor)

Distance from Floor to Bottom of Window Height of Window Including Trim

	Distance from Floor to Bottom of Window	**Height of Window Including Trim**
Window #1:	(inches)	(inches)
Window #2:	(inches)	(inches)
Window #3:	(inches)	(inches)
Window #4:	(inches)	(inches)
Window #5:	(inches)	(inches)
Window #6:	(inches)	(inches)

STEP 4
A) Beginning at the top left of your drawing, label the windows "Window #1", "Window #2", etc. in a clockwise order.

B) Again, beginning at the top left of your drawing, label the doors "Door #1", "Door #2", etc. in a clockwise order.

C) Next to each wall, write the name of the adjacent room. If the wall is an "outside wall" write "exterior wall."

STEP 5
A) Measure any obstructions such as radiators, pipes, etc. that you either can not, or do not, want moved. If the obstruction is close to a wall, measure out from the wall to the edge of the obstruction.

B) Measure from the second closest wall to the edge of the obstruction.

C) If the obstruction does not span the full height of the room, measure the height of the obstruction.

FINAL STEP
Check your measurements. If your room is rectangular add up the measurements of the parallel walls and make sure they match (or are at least very close). For example, in our sample drawing, you would take the overall measurements of the top wall and add them together. Then do the same with the bottom wall. Once you have added each walls measurements check the totals to see if they match.

Top Wall:	24" + 42" + 24" + 12" + 42" + 12" = 156"
Bottom Wall:	12" + 40" + 104" = 156"
Left Wall:	21" + 42" + 52" = 115"
Right Wall:	18" + 97" = 115"

34   Creating Your New Kitchen

If you'd like to do a bit of drawing yourself, you may want to look at the plans below for basic ideas. But keep them to yourself when you visit vendors. Let each make suggestions based on the space plan you've created. Then, incorporate the best of their ideas into your final plan.

The National Kitchen and Bath Association urges those planning new kitchens to conform to a number of standards:

- Stay within the work triangle, an imaginary line drawn from the center of the sink to the center to the center of the cooktop to the center of the refrigerator and back to the sink. The line should be no more than 26 feet in total length with no leg of the triangle shorter than four feet or longer than nine. The triangle should not intersect an island or peninsula by more than 12 inches. If the kitchen has one sink, it should be across from the cooking surface, preparation area or refrigerator.

- Make the kitchen convenient for cooks of different heights by providing for two work-counter heights – one between 28 and 36 inches above the floor; the other between 36 and 45 inches above the floor.

- Be certain that entry, appliance and cabinet doors don't block one another. Appliance or cabinet doors in islands should not hit those across from the island.

- Enhance convenience by adding at least five organizing features such as roll-out shelves, lowered wall cabinets, raised base cabinets, tall cabinets, appliance garages, storage bins, cutlery dividers or swing-out pantries.

- Place microwave ovens in keeping with the primary cook's physical needs, usually between 24 and 48 inches above the floor.

- Include window and/or skylight areas equal to at least 10 percent of the total kitchen area.

Within basic guidelines designed to create optimum ease of use, kitchen designs vary with individual tastes and – where kitchens are to be renovated – limitations imposed by available space and structural components.

Following are several basic designs often used individually or in combination in contemporary homes and in kitchen remodeling projects.

The galley or walk-through kitchen

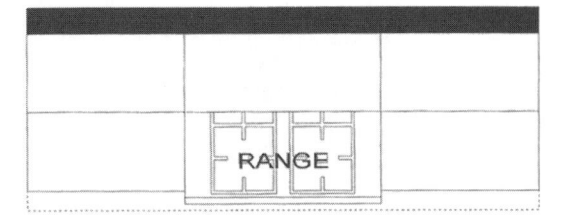

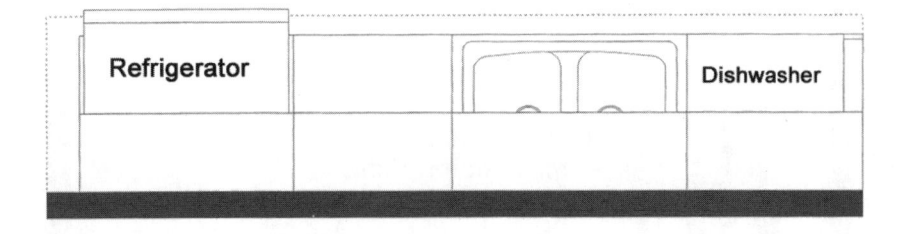

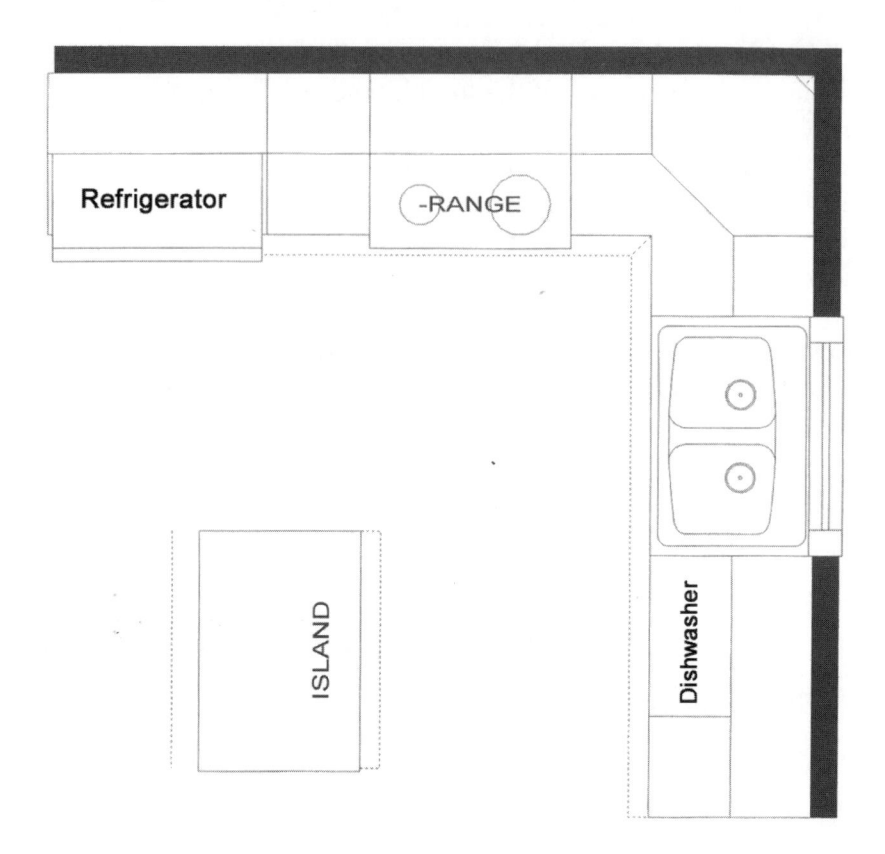

The 'L'- shaped kitchen can be designed with or without island

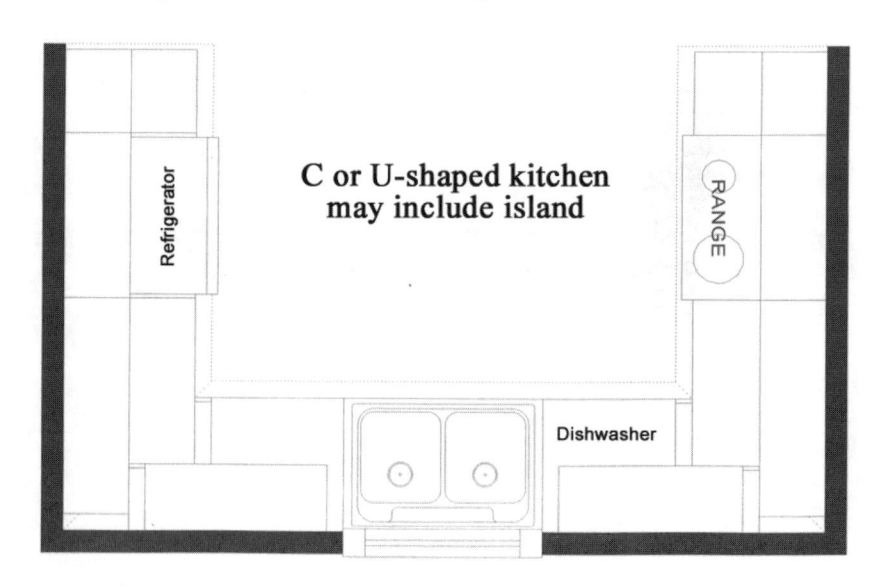

C or U-shaped kitchen may include island

Chapter 6
Islands

The evolution of the kitchen from a place in which food is prepared to an extension of the home's entertainment area has compounded demand for space and work area. The result, in part, has been an explosion of interest in kitchen 'islands.'

These can be as simple or as complex as the homeowner prefers. They range from a simple butcher block or roll-around table to a built-in unit incorporating a sink, dishwasher and other appliances.

Islands can be used to provide:

- Additional counter space.

- A second sink.

- Appliances such as a dishwasher, cooktop, microwave or ovens.

- A raised counter to serve as a snack bar.

- An anchor for a second work triangle in a two-cook kitchen.

- A divider between a kitchen and adjacent living area.

The National Kitchen and Bath Association's guidelines for island planning specify:

- Aisles and passageways should be at least 42 inches wide for a one-cook kitchen; 48 inches wide where two cooks will be working. Passageways not used as work aisles should be at least 36 inches wide.

- Where used as food preparation centers, islands should incorporate at least 36 inches of workspace for each cook and be positioned adjacent to a full size or bar sink.

- Where cooktops or ranges are incorporated into islands, at least nine inches of counter space should be provided on one side; 15 inches on the other.

- Where islands are used for seating, allow at least 24 inches of counter space per seat. A 30-inch high table requires 19 inches of knee room; a 36-inch high table requires 15 inches; a 42-inch high table requires 12 inches.

Notes

Chapter 7
Special Needs

No one should embark upon designing a kitchen today without considering what have been called "special needs." These are design characteristics that can be incorporated into a kitchen to best serve the needs of those whose physical abilities are limited as a result of handicap or age.

If any member of your family falls into one of these categories – or may meet the specified criteria at some future date – your kitchen planning should be undertaken with that factor in mind. Among elements you then may want to include in the kitchen:

- Adjustable counters or counters of varying heights.

- Lighting fixtures to compensate for differences in vision.

- Counter space between appliances to permit pots and pans to be moved by sliding rather than lifting.

- Faucets with lever-type controls of built-in sensors.

- Appliances raised off the floor to minimize back strain.

- Under-counter drawers rather than tall pantries.

- Pull-out storage bins.

- Easy-to-grasp cabinet hardware.

- Child safety devices.

- Strategically-placed controls for all appliances.
- Extra-wide aisles for those who may be wheelchair-bound.

- A wall range rather than a conventional oven.

- Refrigerated drawers rather than a conventional refrigerator.

Notes

Part III
Cabinetry

Selecting cabinetry is one of the most challenging tasks you'll face in building a new home or renovating an existing kitchen. Species of wood, variety in designs and a broad range of quality levels make the task time-consuming and difficult under the best of circumstances.

There nevertheless are a few techniques you can use to separate the wheat from the chaff and the sheep from the goats, as it were.

First, decide how much quality you need. If you're renovating a kitchen you expect to use for the rest of your life, quality is important. If you're merely enhancing appearances in a home you're planning to sell, you can accept something less than the best available.

Second, learn how to differentiate between good and bad – especially in terms of construction. The National Kitchen and Bath Association's web site [www.nkba.org] offers detailed information about cabinet construction. Similar trade association resources provide similar guidance in other areas.

Third, apply the knowledge you've gained in *all* circumstances. Don't be fooled by "the tricks of the trade." For example, a leading furniture manufacturer has licensed the company's name to a cabinet manufacturer to produce a line of "branded" cabinets under the furniture maker's trade name. The only relationship between the furniture company and the cabinet company is a contract governing the use of the name.

Another example: a leading design firm has licensed it's name to a cabinet manufacturer who, in turn, is providing "exclusive designer cabinets" to one of the nation's leading building supply stores. Again, the only relationship that exists between the design firm and the cabinets is the contract covering use of the name.

Moral: make it your business to know the difference between high and low quality cabinets, and select those that best meet your needs. Or contract with a reliable source to do the job for you.

Notes

Chapter 8
Selecting Cabinetry

Selecting cabinets for a new kitchen is a complex task. The homeowner or homebuyer must make a long series of choices. They're not hard to deal with when taken in logical sequence. Handled otherwise, they can produce confusion and frustration.

The decisions involve choosing from among:

Three types of cabinets – stock, semi-custom and custom. Quality varies within each category. All are factory-produced. They differ in quality of workmanship and materials, in price, and in the extent to which they are customized for the kitchen.

Construction and assembly are major factors in establishing the quality of kitchen cabinetry. Construction methods are framed or frameless. Materials may be solid woods or laminates; plywood, flakeboard, or fiberboard; thick or thin. Assembly can be accomplished with staples, screws, glues or combinations of these elements.

Wood species and non-wood options. Species usually are selected for their color and grain patterns. The most popular are cherry, hickory, maple, walnut, oak and pine, but others are used as well. Polyester, plastic laminates and stainless steel are among common cabinet materials.

Door types and styles. Types include inset, lipped, partial overlay or full overlay. The major styles are recessed panel, raised panel, curved panel, beadboard panel and flat slab.

Door finishes, including stain, paint, polyester, plastic laminate, stainless steel and glass.

Drawer materials, assembly methods, support systems and guides.

Pulls and knobs, which are available in an almost limitless range of types and styles.

Accessories to enhance ease of access or user convenience. These include rollout, foldout, swing-out and rotary shelves as well as bins, drawer dividers, wine and plate racks and other special-purpose features.

Where do you begin? With none of the above! Think first about who's going to use the kitchen, for what purpose, and for how long.

Families with children tend to over-buy in terms of quality. The useful life of the best [and most expensive] drawers in the world may be measured in months where youngsters use them as ladders to reach wall cabinets.

Empty nesters usually over-buy in quantity. They've often been traumatized by rearing children in too-small kitchens and compensate by enlarging beyond the needs of almost any couple.

Confused? Don't despair. We're going to guide you through each of these jungles, help you through the decision-making processes, and see that you come as close as possible to obtaining the kitchen you want at a price you can afford within the time frame you've established.

A few basic guidelines before we begin:

- Limit base cabinets to 24-inches in depth – the size at which they'll accommodate appliances such as dishwashers and provide more work surface.

- Place tall units, such as those that house ovens, at the end of base cabinet runs rather than between conventional base units to avoid breaking up work surfaces.

- Position wall units at least 15 to 18 inches above work surfaces so that you'll always be able to see all of the work surface.

Creating Your New Kitchen 45

- Be careful placing cabinets in corners to ensure that doors don't open into one another.

- Place food storage centers adjacent to refrigerators and away from heat and steam. Use wall cupboards for dry goods and make provision to store cleaning materials separately.

- Knives, strainers, graters, and other utensils should be stored in the preparation area near the sink. So, too, should the garbage bin and any recycling bins.

- Provide deep drawers or cupboards in the cooking area for pots and pans, baking dishes, etc. Wall racks and/or shallow drawers should be used for cooking utensils.

- Exercise care in dealing with corners. Angled cabinets are advisable. In the alternative, consider a bi-fold door, a revolving carousel unit, a single door with two lazy Susan trays, or a single cupboard next to a compartment for trays or wines.

- Add cabinet space by using tall wall cabinets.

Notes

Notes

Chapter 9
Types of Cabinets

Creating or renovating kitchens – as suggested earlier – involves three major variables: speed, quality and price. You can select any two of the three. Looking at it another way, you're going to have to sacrifice in one area or another – perhaps in several -- beginning with your choice of cabinet type.

> **Custom** cabinets offer the greatest range of design options – colors, finishes, decorations, and sizes. They're the most expensive cabinets available, however, and require more lead time in manufacturing. Buyers win on quality but lose on cost as well as time factors.
>
> **Semi-custom** cabinets provide some flexibility in finishes and dimensions. Quality tends to be a bit lower than in custom cabinetry, however, and cost is significantly lower. Delivery is quicker.
>
> **In stock** cabinets, what you see is what you get. You can select from among the finishes, sizes and features offered. Delivery of stock cabinets usually is somewhat more rapid than for the semi-custom and custom varieties but "stock" usually means stock in a manufacturer's warehouse rather than at your local dealership. If you select a popular product that's in the warehouse you can expect delivery in a matter of weeks. Price and quality will be lower than is the case in semi-custom and custom lines.

As with most things one buys, however, the real world is more complicated than it appears. We live in a society in which the lowest price is not always the best price. More important, manufacturers no longer are as rigorous in protecting brand names, as once was the case.

Determining whether the lowest price is best requires the ability to …

- Examine the product involved.

- Compare physical attributes.

- Draw accurate conclusions as to whether quality has been sacrificed to achieve the lower price.

Consumers once were able to take some comfort in the reputation of merchants or products – in brand names. Unfortunately, this is no longer the case. Many manufacturers are willing to compromise their standards to expand market share.

In cabinetry, this phenomenon is most often seen in the outlets of national chain stores offering brand name merchandise manufactured to retailer standards. In power tools, for example, national hardware/home store chains offer product models found nowhere else. Almost invariably, products that appear identical in gross terms – horsepower ratings, for example – have been altered in other ways to permit their being sold at "low warehouse" prices.

Comparison shoppers have found that cabinetry prices in so-called "big box" stores often are markedly higher than those of locally-owned specialty stores. The "allegedly low warehouse prices," in addition, often are accompanied by business practices that create contingent problems for customers. Requests for full payment in advance or for large deposits are not uncommon.

Another important point of difference: Specialty stores usually provide "turn-key" services through their own installation technicians and service personnel. Mass merchandisers usually sub-contract their installation work. Quality can vary as a result. More important, problems in material or workmanship may be difficult to resolve after merchant and installer have been paid.

Those planning new homes or kitchen renovations therefore should follow a logical step-by-step planning process.

1. Select the type of cabinetry you want – custom, semi-custom or stock.

2. Examine vendors' offerings within the category selected.

3. Make basic choices based on quality of construction.

4. Make design and color choices based on personal criteria.

Notes

Notes

Chapter 10
Cabinet Construction

Quality in cabinetry begins with the materials used in basic construction and the ways in which they are assembled. The superficial attributes – colors and style – are important to the consumer, but durability begins with the basics.

A cabinet consists of two components: the box and the doors and/or drawers. The box, as it's called, is produced in one of two forms: framed and frameless.

Framed cabinets are held together through traditional wood joinery. Vertical stiles and horizontal rails attach the door to the box. Special hardware accomplishes the same objective in frameless cabinets.

The two approaches differ significantly in only one respect from the consumer viewpoint: The absence of rails and stiles makes access a bit easier.

The box is fabricated using one or more of three materials:

- Plywood.

- Particleboard or flakeboard.

- Fiberboard.

These materials are used rather than solid woods in that they are resistant to warping – a significant factor in kitchens, baths and other areas in which humidity levels can vary from hour to hour. Plywood is most durable and holds wood screws best. Synthetic additives strengthen the plywood substitutes -- flakeboard, particleboard and fiberboard. Some finishes perform better on one material than another, however, so the absence of plywood is not necessarily a sign of manufacturer "corner-cutting."

Boxes should be fabricated of thick panels [the best are three quarter inch] attached at their corners by block-and-glue and/or wood screws. Staples or nails in boxes or drawers should be avoided in that they pull out too easily.

Solid woods, rarely used in cabinet boxes because of their tendency to warp, may be applied in face frames, doors and exposed side panels. Doors often are fabricated of solid woods. Face frames and side panels usually are finished in matching veneers.

Warping is discouraged in solid wood doors by fabricating them of multiple strips of wood in a variety of sizes rather than in one piece. Doors also may be constructed of frames and "floating panels." The latter are fitted into grooves in the frames rather than glued, allowing them to "float" with changes in humidity.

Notes

Chapter 11
Door and Drawers - Types and Styles

Cabinet doors are fabricated in four basic types and five basic styles. Type refers to the manner in which the doors are attached to cabinet boxes. Style refers to the design of the door's front surface.

Types of doors used on kitchen cabinetry are inset, lipped, partial overlay and full overlay:

- Inset doors are positioned flush with the front of the cabinet box, within rails and styles.

- Lipped doors shaped with wooden grooves that fit over face frames.

- Partial overlay doors conceal some but not all of the box frame.

- Full overlay doors are fitted with less than an eighth of an inch between them to fully cover the frame.

All frameless cabinets come with full overlay doors, as do some framed cabinets. The type of cabinet becomes evident when the door is opened.

Cabinet doors are offered in five basic styles although a single manufacturer may offer hundreds of variations on the basic themes, all with matching drawer fronts:

- Recessed panel.

- Raised panel.

- Curved panel.

- Beadboard panel.

- Flat slab.

Most door styles are available in almost infinite combinations of materials and finishes. The most popular materials are:

- Wood
- Wood veneer
- Plastic laminate
- Stainless steel
- Glass

Finishes include:

- Stain
- Glaze
- Paint
- Polyester
- Varnish

Wood and wood veneer typically are stained and then varnished. Catalytic conversion varnishes typically are used because they catalyze into hard, protective finishes upon baking. Oil, lacquer and wax are avoided in that they yellow over time. Glazes often are added to provide special paint effects such as an antique look.

Paint produces base colors and special effects in virtually any shade. Paint can dry smooth and glossy and then can be sanded, rubbed or otherwise tortured to provide a distressed appearance. There is, however, one drawback in the use of paint on solid wood doors. Hairline cracks usually appear at door joints as the wood expands and contracts. Those who want painted doors often elect to substitute medium density fiberboard for wood to avoid the cracking problem.

Polyester resins, long used in automobile finishes, also are available from some cabinet vendors. The product – in glossy and matte finishes -- fills pores to create an ultra smooth surface. As many as 20 steps may be involved, including applying a top coat in a dust-free environment, before special polishes are used to produce mirror-like final finish.

Plastic laminates are the same materials used in many countertops. Available in an almost limitless array of colors, patterns and textures, they're stain-resistant and easy to clean. Plastic laminates can chip, however, and the chips are difficult to repair. In addition, because the material consists largely of paper – kraft paper topped with a decorative paper and a plastic coating – most laminates have a brown edge. Solid color laminates fabricated from colored paper are available but at higher cost.

Stainless steel is relatively rare in residential cabinetry but common in commercial kitchens. In most cases, relatively thin steel is wrapped around a core of wood or another material to add weight and dampen "tinny" sounds. Fingerprints and scratches stand out, however, on the sleek, commercial kitchen look that results.

All materials used in doors also can be used in drawers. Most drawers have framed or slab fronts and are held together by dovetail, mortise-and-tenon, or butt joints. Doors fastened only with staples or nails should be avoided.

Drawers differ primarily in hardware rather than material. Drawer slide alternatives are:

- Full extension, where slides are attached to drawer bottoms or sides to provide full access to interiors. Ball bearings add strength and stability and heavier versions are used on drawers designed for files or cookware.

- Ball bearing slides attached to the bottoms of drawer sides for smooth operation. Concealed runners stay cleaner than those on drawer sides and permit drawer boxes to be widened to produce more usable space inside.

- Track and roller slides [epoxy-coated steel tracks and nylon rollers] attach to drawer sides and are quieter but less stable than those in which ball bearings are used.

- Wood slides are similar to those used in wooden furniture and run through slots in drawer bottoms or sides. They've declined in popularity because the expansion and contraction of wood can make drawers stick.

Notes

Chapter 12
Accessories

When your basic kitchen design is complete and cabinetry has been selected, you'll want to consider the many accessories made available by most cabinet manufacturers. The most popular among them include:

- Towel rails concealed behind what appear to be cabinet doors.

- Cutlery tray inserts to make drawers more useful.

- Pull-out ironing boards hidden behind dummy drawer fronts.

- Garbage bins attached to the inside of a base cabinet door.

- Recycling bins, usually on pull-out fixtures in base cabinets.

- Baskets for produce – wire or plastic – in lieu of base cabinet shelves.

- Pull-out drawers behind base cabinet doors.

- Carousel shelves – wood, wire, or plastic – mounted inside base and wall cabinets to better use corner space.

- Pull-out tables.

- Swing-up mixer or blender supports not unlike the concealed typewriter wells once contained in most desks.

- Wine storage shelves.

- Toe-kick drawers to capture otherwise-wasted space beneath base cabinets.

- Décor panels that match cabinets to conceal dishwashers and other appliances.

- Mid-range [between wall and base cabinets] cupboards and/or and shallow shelves.

- Mid-range swing-down chopping boards.

- Tall cabinets to serve as pantries, storage for cleaning implements and cleansers, etc.

- Spice racks incorporated into drawers or placed on the inside of cabinet doors.

- Swing-down book rests positioned beneath wall cabinets for cookbooks.

- Open shelf units often used at the ends of cabinet runs.

Notes

Chapter 13
Space-Saving Ideas

You can never have too much space in a kitchen. Neither can you have too many space-savers. The following list is necessarily incomplete – someone's coming up with something new every day – but you'll nevertheless find some ideas you can use.

- Use tall wall cabinets to expand total storage space.

- Provide space for a folding stool to make tall cabinets easier to reach.

- Consider using a wall-mounted microwave to conserve work surface.

- Put cutlery in shallow, divided drawers or use free-standing cutlery racks.

- Hang cups on hooks between wall and base cabinets

- Use a magnetic wall-mounted knife rack.

- Attach pegboard to inside of cabinet doors to hang utensils.

- Install toe-kick drawers beneath cabinets for seldom-used items.

- Use a counter top appliance garage for items such as mixers and toasters.

- Consider adding "midway units" between wall and base cabinets – shallow shelves, racks, hanging rails and boxes.

- Pull-out wire or plastic baskets in base cabinets maximize usable space.

- Use space above cabinets for rarely-used pots and pans.

- Add ceiling-mounted racks above islands for hanging storage.

- In planning, make certain you've provided space for:
    o Fresh and frozen food.
    o Canned and packaged food.
    o Pots, pans and utensils.
    o Small appliances.
    o Ovenware.
    o China and glassware.
    o Table linen.
    o Cutlery.
    o Plastic bags, foil, plastic wrap, etc.
    o Cleaning equipment and supplies.
    o Garbage and recycling bins.

Notes

Chapter 14
Hardware

You've managed to find your way through hundreds of cabinet and door styles. You've breathed a sigh of relief. The worst appears to be over. But that's not quite the case.

You're going to find that there are at least as many variations in cabinet hardware as there are in cabinets. In addition, drawer pulls and hinges range in cost from pennies to $100 or more – each!

Knobs and pulls are available in:

- Metals, including brass, bronze, aluminum, and stainless steel.

- Resins and solid surface materials of the sort used in countertops.

- Ceramics, often with hand-decorated finishes.

- Wood – stained or painted.

- Glass and crystal, clear or colored.

The range of possibilities is almost limitless. You can select hardware to:

- Reflect the part of the country in which your home is located.

- Coordinate with wall coverings or window treatments.

- Repeat the dominant color in your china.

- Express your vocational or avocational interests.

62 *Creating Your New Kitchen*

- Compliment cabinetry or appliances.

Notes

Wood·Mode
FINE CUSTOM CABINETRY

Wood-Mode
FINE CUSTOM CABINETRY

Wood-Mode
FINE CUSTOM CABINETRY

Wood-Mode
FINE CUSTOM CABINETRY

Wood-Mode
FINE CUSTOM CABINETRY

Wood-Mode
FINE CUSTOM CABINETRY

Wood·Mode
FINE CUSTOM CABINETRY

Wood-Mode
FINE CUSTOM CABINETRY

Wood-Mode
FINE CUSTOM CABINETRY

CARDELL
CABINETRY

Kitchen Craft
CABINETRY

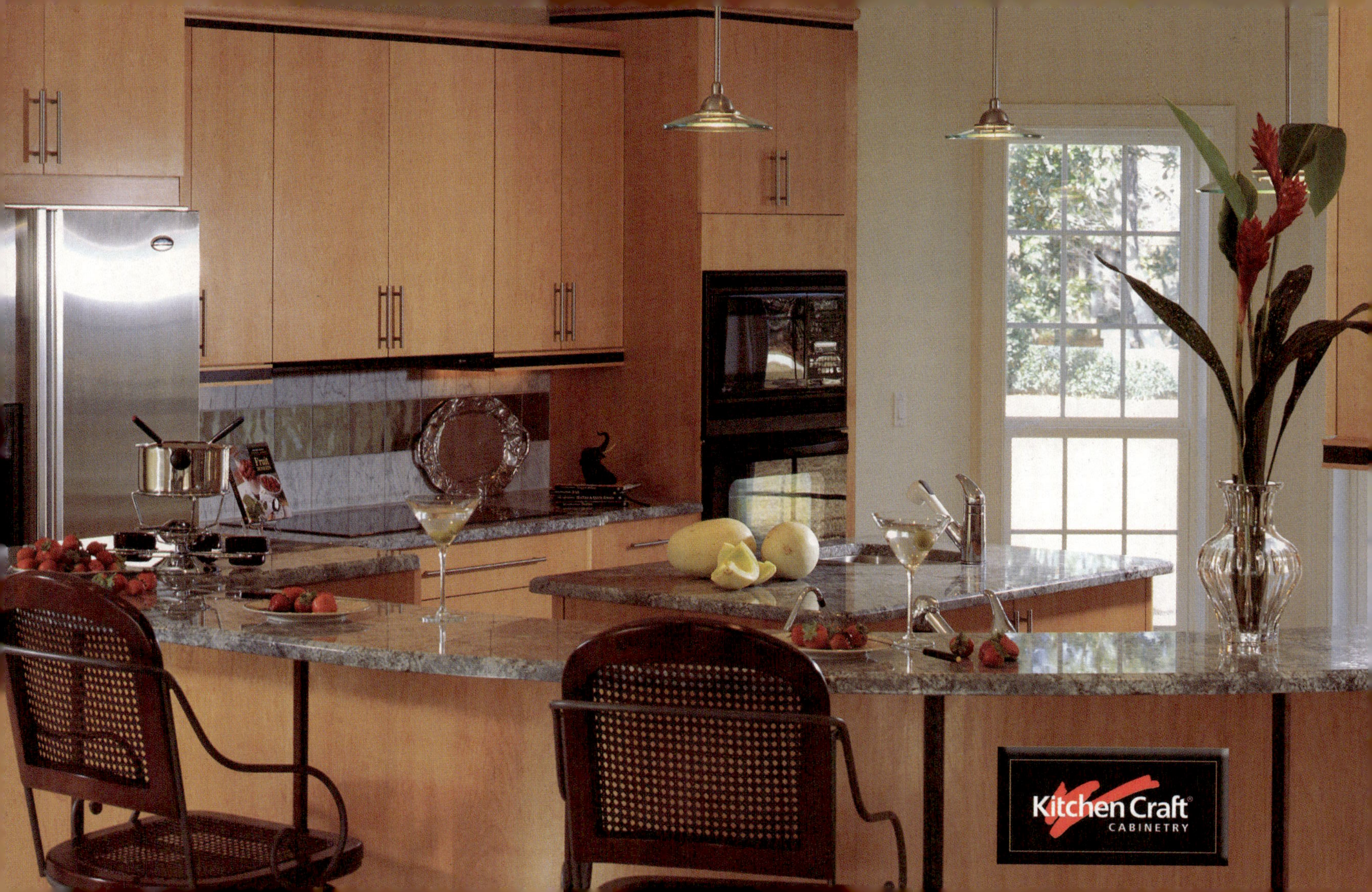
Kitchen Craft®
CABINETRY

Kitchen Craft
CABINETRY

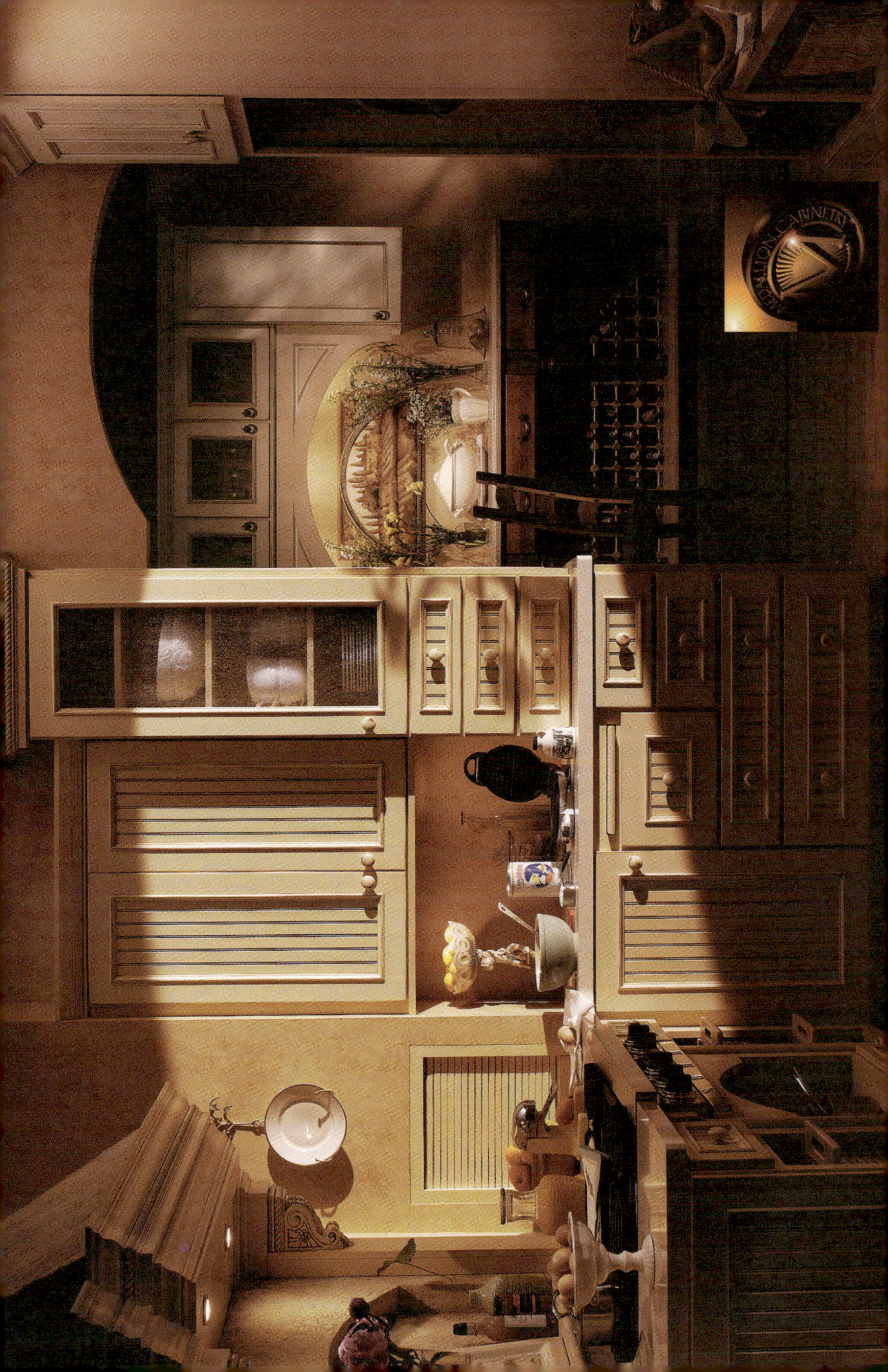
MEDALLION CABINETRY

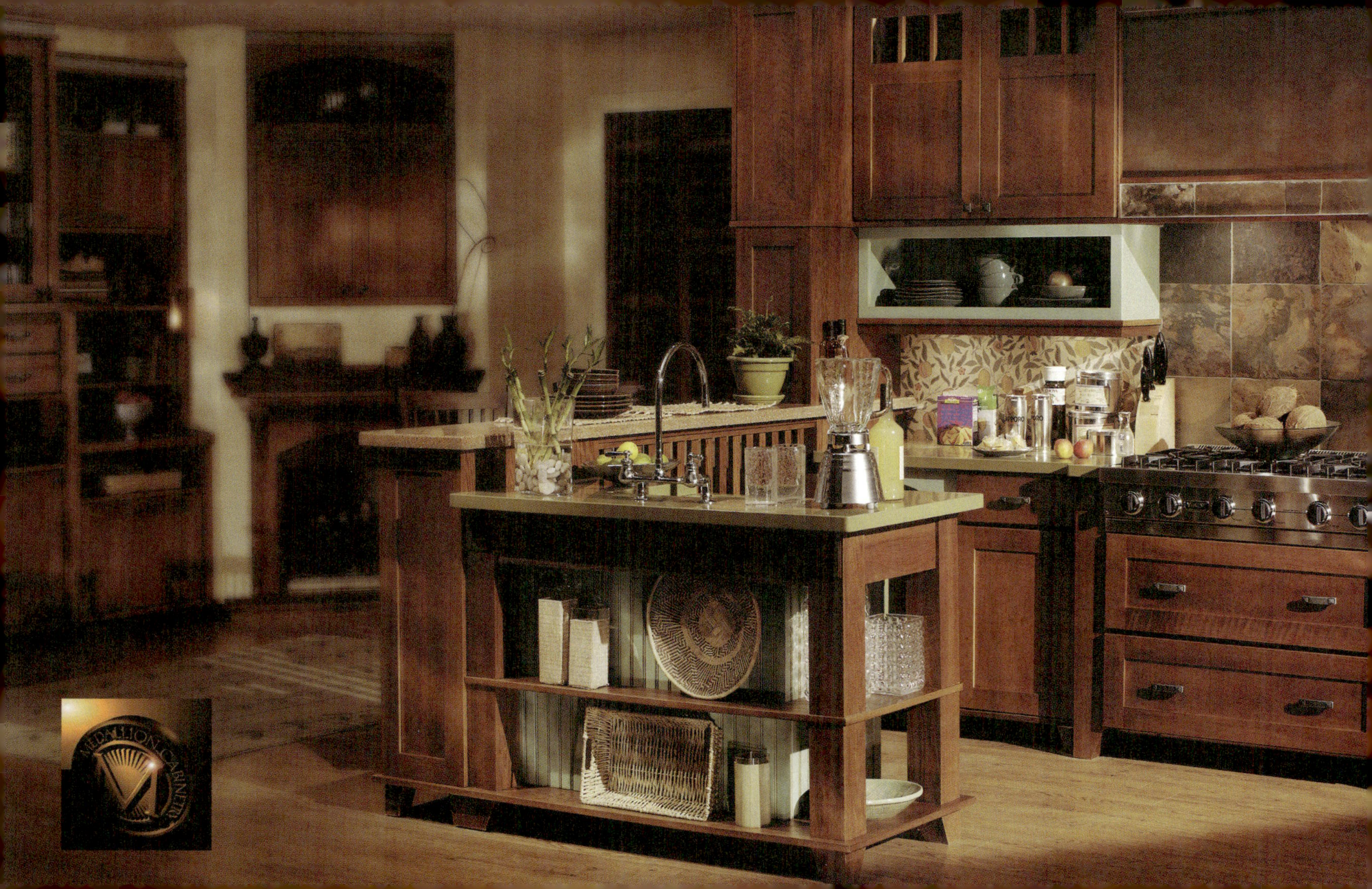
MEDALLION CABINETRY

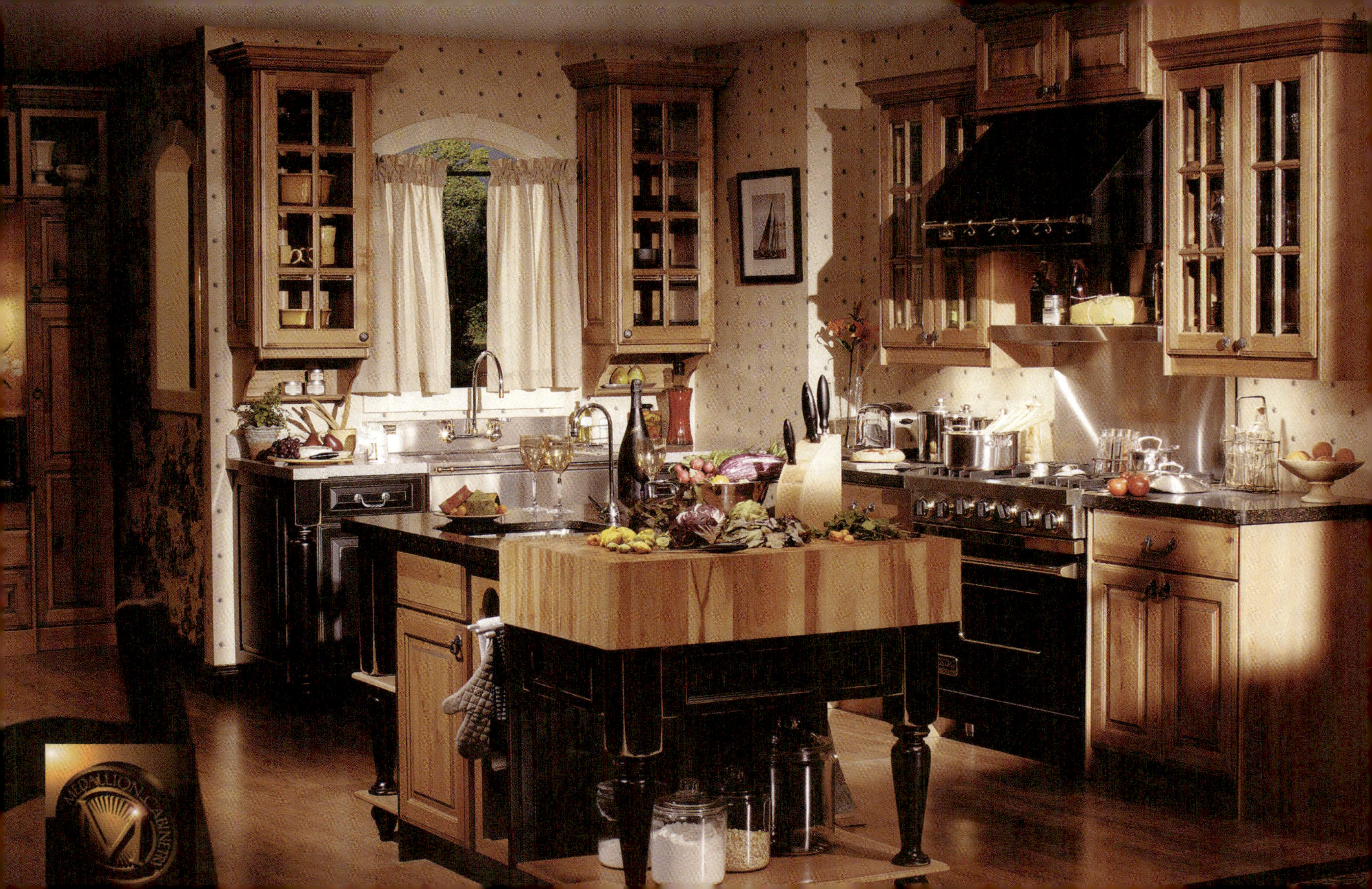
MEDALLION CABINETRY

Section IV
Other Products and Materials

Cabinetry is by far the largest component of the kitchen in quantity and in value. You're going to buy more of it and spend more on it than you'll dedicate to any other sector.

But while cabinetry makes the kitchen, the other elements are equally important and each demands close attention if your finished kitchen is to become everything you want it to be. Among the "ingredients" with which you should be concerned:

- Countertops
- Appliances
- Sinks and faucets
- Flooring
- Lighting
- Architectural detail
- Walls and ceilings
- Windows and doors
- Moldings and trim
- One-of-a-kind items

We'll examine each of these categories in the chapters that follow.

Notes

Chapter 15
Countertops

Countertops, until relatively recently, were available in any material you wanted as long as it was laminate. And you could have any one of a few dozen solid colors.

No longer! Today you first choose from among a half dozen material options and then have to deal with an almost unlimited number of colors, patterns and designs. Your options:

- Laminate
- Wood
- Tile
- Concrete
- Solid surface
- Stone
- Stainless steel

Each of these materials has attributes and drawbacks.

Durability is greatest in solid surface and stone. Cleanup is easiest with solid surfaces or stainless steel. The greatest range of colors and patterns is available in laminates and solid surfaces. Decorative shapes and integral sinks are attributes of solid surfaces and stainless steel.

Many homeowners today opt for multiple materials. Example: granite serving island, solid surface tops for food preparation and tile backsplashes. You'll want to consider the attributes of each.

Laminate is produced in hundreds of colors, patterns and finishes. It's easy to maintain and impact-resistant but subject to chipping. Heat and water seeping into seams can produce delamination – layers breaking apart. The material is fabricated of multiple layers of kraft papers [much like grocery bags] and a melamine plastic coating.

Butcher block is made of laminated strips of hardwoods such as maple or oak. It won't dull knife blades but requires regular resealing, shows knife marks and is prone to water damage.

Decorative tile – often used for trim and backsplashes but seldom for counter tops – comes in ceramic [made from pressed clay with a matte finish or glaze], porcelain [baked at higher temperatures with color all the way through] and quarry [an unglazed tile made from a shale and clay mix]. Space between tiles is filled with grout – preferably an epoxy grout that resists stains – in almost any color.

Concrete is a hardened mixture of water, cement, and sand and/or gravel that can be pre-cast or cast on site in almost any shape. Lacquer sealers and glass tops help prevent stains and water damage. Concrete can be fashioned in a variety of textures and dyes can be used to add color. The material resists scratches but stains easily and can crack or crumble.

Solid surfaces are fashioned from synthetic sheets formed by mixing a mineral compound with a polyester or acrylic resin. Finished materials are available in a broad range of colors and finishes and can be shaped to create decorative forms and integral sinks. Chips, dents and scratches are easily repaired but the material can crack while cooling after a hot item has been placed on it. Stains are easily removed but sharp impacts can cause discoloration and a cutting board is necessary to prevent scratching.

Natural stone such as granite, marble, limestone, Jerusalem stone, and natural quartz are often used in kitchen counters. All are porous and require sealing and regular resealing. Granite is most durable. Marble is a favorite surface for rolling dough. Limestone and Jerusalem stone offer a weathered look but are softer and more porous.

Natural quartz has a slate-like appearance and does not stain or scratch easily. Caution: colors vary. Users should inspect material selected for their kitchens before it is fabricated.

Engineered quartz is fabricated from natural stone [more than 90 percent] and resin binders, providing the look of natural stone with a consistent color.

Stainless steel is an alloy containing chromium to make it rust-resistant. Typically attached to plywood or particleboard backing for added strength and to eliminate "tinny" sounds, stainless steel won't stain, cleans easily, and can incorporate an integral sink. The material shows scratches and fingerprints, however, and is subject to denting.

Deciding on the "best" material for your kitchen involves weighing the attributes of all of them and sorting out those you consider most important. Do you want:

- Smooth or textured?
- Ease of cleaning?
- An integral sink?
- Consistency in color?
- Natural or manmade?
- Freedom from cutting boards?
- Something tolerant of hot pots?
- Freedom from resealing?
- Resistance to spills and stains?

You can have each, but not all. Solid surfaces and stone are most durable. Stone and stainless steel are most spill-resistant. Stone and wood serve best for rolling dough and as cutting boards. Laminates offer the broadest range of colors and patterns. Integral sinks are available in solid surface, stainless steel and concrete. On the down side, steel scratches and shows fingerprints. Tile creates a rough surface and grout can stain. Wood requires resealing. Concrete stains easily.

If you have difficulty making up your mind, consider mixing two or more materials to achieve the mix of utilitarian factors you're seeking.

Where space is at a premium, you also may want to consider adding a roll-around trolley or work stand that can be hidden in a closet when not needed.

Similarly, a pull-out table can fit into a drawer space and extended to provide additional counter space or to serve as a table.

Notes

Chapter 16
Appliances

If you think selecting cabinets is difficult, wait until you wade into the appliance jungle. You're going to have to sort out ovens, cooktops, ranges, refrigerators, dishwashers, ventilation units and a host of specialty items ranging from wine coolers to icemakers.

You'll find categories of products within each of the basic groups and multiple options within each category. Do you want:

- Professional or standard?

- Built-in, paneled or free-standing?

- With what specific features?

"Professional" refers to style rather than type. Commercial equipment used in restaurants requires special ventilation systems to cope with heat output and massive size. Professional-style appliances are built to restaurant quality standards and provide greater durability, better temperature controls, and stainless steel finishes. They're great for large families but otherwise are purchased more for appearance than utilitarian value.

Standard appliances also come in stainless steel should that be what you prefer, but there are other options that also should be considered. Most important among them will be your decision as to whether you want appliances built into your cabinets, paneled or free-standing.

Built-in appliances are not immediately identifiable as what they are. They look like over-size cabinets. Paneled appliances' doors are customized to match your cabinetry while the free-standing version come without such luxury touches.

The range of options is broad and gets progressively broader. You can have refrigerators and freezers in drawers under your counters rather than standing in the usual configuration. There are brick ovens for pizza lovers and beverage chillers for wine aficionados. The list is almost endless, and the problem is compounded by the number of types in each category.

Ovens, for example, are available in conventional, convection, microwave, combination and specialty types.

- Conventional ovens are heated by electromagnetic waves radiating from the oven's sides. Heat is generated at the bottom and rises to the top, which makes for uneven heating.

- Convection ovens generate more even heat. A fan – which can be noisy – recirculates air. Cookbook cooking times may have to be reduced to avoid overcooking.

- Microwave ovens cook by rapidly moving water molecules in the food with an alternating electronic field. Those that operate at 750 to 1000 watts are most efficient. Microwave ovens cook food rapidly. Overcooking is common, however, and food doesn't brown as it does in other ovens.

- Combination ovens incorporate multiple heating methods. You can buy a conventional oven with a convection option, or a microwave oven with a halogen light unit that can reduce baking times by 75 percent. You get greater flexibility and higher costs.

- Specialty ovens now available range from the brick pizza oven mentioned earlier to warming drawers equipped with humidifiers and designed to keep food at desired temperatures without drying it out.

Cooktops or ranges are available in similarly diverse models. You can have gas burners, electric coils, glass ceramic surfaces [usually heated by electric coils] or modular burners.

- Gas burners give you instant heat and more precise temperature control but require gas connections.

- Electric coils don't pollute and are easier to maintain and repair but electricity can cost more than gas and temperature control is more difficult.

- Glass ceramic surfaces heated by radiant, halogen or magnetic induction elements are easy to clean and can contribute to counter space when not in use but it's difficult to tell when they're hot and temperature controls are imprecise.

- Modular burners typically are equipped with downdraft exhaust systems making them more flexible in use but more difficult to clean.

Range options include freestanding, slide-in and drop-in types. Oven and cooktop typically use the same energy source.

- Freestanding units sit between cabinets and typically have a bottom drawer and controls on the back of the unit. They usually are least expensive but crumbs and liquids can fall into cracks between the range and the cabinets.

- Slide-in units eliminate the gap. Their controls are situated in the front.

- Drop-ins are suspended on the countertop and appear to be built in. They require support from below and front paneling below the unit.

In selecting ovens, make certain that:

- Shelf supports prevent their tipping when partly pulled out.

- Glass doors permit your seeing food while it's cooking.

- Oven lights illuminate interiors.

- Hinged doors are reversible – hinges can be hung from either side.

- Drop-down doors are strong enough to support a Thanksgiving turkey and are tipped slightly inward to prevent pans from slipping off.

- Removable doors and linings are easily cleaned.

- Self-cleaning oven linings vaporize food splashes at low to medium settings.

- Controls are easy to reach.

Ventilation devices come in two varieties – updraft and downdraft. The updraft devices typically are housed in hoods and the downdraft are in cabinets below. You'll want to consider at least five factors in making your selection:

- Canopy size, which must be adequate to the dimensions of your cooktop.

- Blower capacity [measured in cubic feet of air handled per minute] and quietness.

- Installation, which should be done by a qualified technician and incorporate ductwork in dimensions specified by the manufacturer.

- Ease of cleaning.

- Fire safety. Centrifuge filtration systems create barriers to flame. A fire that breaks out on your range would not be able to reach your attic.

Basic types of hoods and differences between them:

- Vent hood fans pull air through filters and exhaust it to the outdoors via a metal duct or return it to the kitchen. Hoods can be decorative but are difficult to keep clean. Filters must be cleaned regularly and fans can be noisy.

- Downdraft units contain blowers that exhaust air by pulling it through vents on the surface of the cooktop. Some are equipped with vents that rise when the cooktop is turned on and drop out of sight at other times. They're relatively efficient in handling air around island cooktops but don't catch steam rising from taller pots and pans.

At least five styles also are available:

- Conventional, wall-mounted units that protrude beyond neighboring cabinets.

- Canopy-style units, usually provided in beaten copper or brass, to complement 'rustic' kitchens.

- Integrated units installed behind a hinged door or dummy front to blend with the cabinetry.

- Telescopic pull-out units, built into a wall.

- Downdraft extractors, installed at counter-top level next to the range.

Refrigerators come in top freezer, bottom freezer, side-by-side and specialty models. All offer a host of features including sliding and adjustable shelves, interior wine racks, in-door chillers, ice-and-water dispenser, and many more.

- Top-freezer models tend to be roomiest and least expensive.

- Bottom-freezer units' refrigerators are more accessible but freezers are less accessible and the design precludes in-door ice and water dispensers.

- Side-by-side model compartments are more accessible but not as energy-efficient and compartments are narrower.

- Specialty models include under-counter refrigerators and freezers, wine chillers and icemakers. Under-counter units can be built into cabinets to provide enhanced access.

You'll want to make certain that your refrigerator includes:

- Salad bins or drawers

- A dairy shelf

- A frozen food compartment

- Interior light

- Beverage and ice dispensers

- Icemaker

- Adjustable feet to alter height.

- Egg storage

- Automatic defrost system

- Shelf for standing bottles

- Warning lights

- Water filtration system.

- High energy efficiency levels to limit power costs.

- Extra-wide shelves for oversized beverage containers.

- Temperature controlled meat lockers to chill meats without freezing them.

- Clear bins and crisper drawers that let you see what's inside.

- Adjustable compartments and shelving that let you customize the interior.

- Shelves that slide in and out [vs. the fixed variety].

- An alarm that indicates when the door is left open.

A free-standing freezer ideally should provide:

- Adjustable feet

- Lockable door(s)

- Interior light

- Automatic defrost

- Baskets

- Drawer compartments

- Fast freeze capability

Dishwashers vary in the ways in which they load, where their controls are located, numbers of wash cycles available, height and placement, cleaning power, noise levels, accessories, and materials.

- Electronic controls have proven to be more reliable over time than mechanical.

- Multiple drawers permit users to segregate fine china from pots and pans.

- Stainless steel and porcelain interiors are more durable than plastics.

Dishwashers come in four types: portable compact, front-loading, built-in compact, and integrated. The latter is a standard machine designed to accommodate a panel that matches cabinet doors. In selecting a dishwasher, you'll want to look for:

- Capacity

- Available space

- A quick wash cycle

- Quietness

- A delay timer

- Childproof controls

- Anti-flood feature

- Easily-removable baskets

- Rinse aid

- Plate size limitations

- Door frame design

- Wash temperatures available

A few suggestions:

Ovens should be positioned at least 12 inches from corners to ensure that doors will open easily and never should be placed within the radius of an inward-opening door. Eye-level units should be placed at the end of a run of cabinets with ample work surface on one side. If your ovens have side-opening doors, their handles should be adjacent to the work surface.

Cooktops should have at least 12 inches of work surface on each side. Gas units should be out of drafts. Exhaust hoods are essential where cooktops are placed below cabinets.

Dishwashers should be near sinks in which plates are rinsed.

Refrigerators and freezers should be positioned so that door hinges are at least four inches from adjacent walls or cabinets.

Sinks and drain surfaces should have a minimum of 40 inches of counter space.

If you're going to us "slot-in" vs. built in appliances, consider placing them on rollers and equipping them with long water and power connections to make cleaning easier.

Notes

Notes

Chapter 17
Sinks and Faucets

Sinks come in four basic varieties – top-mounted or self-rimming, under-mounted, integral, and apron or farmhouse. The latter design incorporates an integral apron of the material in which the sink is fabricated. The apron may be plain or decorated and the unit sits atop a cabinet unit.

Selecting from among only four sink types should make the decision-making easy. But it doesn't.

Why? Because the under-mounted and integral sinks that make cleaning easier also impose limitations as to materials. And because sink manufacturers have developed a large number of design variations to complicate the decision-making process.

Integral sinks, which offer smooth visual transitions from countertop to sink – as well as easy cleaning – can be had in only three materials: solid surface, composite and stainless steel. Top-mounted sinks create no such limitations but their rims make cleaning a bit more difficult.

Stainless steel, the most popular of sink materials, is equally at home in contemporary and traditional kitchens. It scratches, however, and while it will eventually develop a patina of its' own, some also consider it "noisy" in that sound-deadening backings are limited.

Some homeowners prefer porcelain-on-iron sinks because they are quieter in use and available in a number of strong designer colors as well as white.

Selecting from among the three functional choices – integral, under-mounted and top-mounted – nevertheless is easier than choosing specific sinks. They come in one-, two- and three-bowl models and in different shapes.

Is one large, deep basin better than two or three smaller ones? If multiple basins are preferred, should they be incorporated into a single sink or would two locations create greater flexibility in the kitchen?

And then there's the matter of accessories and faucets. The former – from soap dispensers and spray hoses to "instant" dispensers of super-heated water – require mounting holes. Their positions are fixed in steel and porcelain sinks but can be positioned as you prefer where integral or bottom-mounted varieties are used.

Let's try to sort things out systematically – beginning with the sinks – self-rimming, under-mounted and integral. Under-mounted and integral make for easy clean-up. There's no rim to catch crumbs en route to the sink. But self-rimming varieties are least expensive.

Sink materials -- Sink materials include stainless steel, enameled cast iron, solid surface and composite. Stainless steel is most popular. It can be molded as part of the countertop, won't chip and is easily cleaned. But it shows scratches and – in lighter weights – dents easily and sounds "tinny."

Enameling can be had on steel or cast iron, which is the stronger and less noisy of the two. Many colors are available but enamel is subject to chipping and staining.

Integral sinks are fashioned of the same material used in the countertops – a mineral compound mixed with polyester or acrylic resins. They can be molded together from a single piece of material and scratches can be sanded out – but they can be damaged by hot pots and pans.

Composite sinks are heat and stain-resistant. They're made from quartz compounds mixed with resins, come in many colors and can be shaped into integral countertops.

Sink configurations – Sinks come in four basic configurations: single, double and triple-bowl and a main sink plus a preparation sink. Where multiple bowls are used, they may or may not be the same size. Triple-bowl models often are designed with two bowls of the same size and a smaller bowl leading to a garbage disposal. Available special features vary with manufacturers but often include:

- Cutting boards that fit within sink openings.

- Colanders that hang on the sides of sinks.

- Dish racks that fit within basins.

Some consider hot water dispensers and garbage disposals to be special features of sinks. In prefabricated sinks, openings for hot water dispensers or other accessories are created in the manufacturing process and can be used for other purposes such as soap or lotion dispensers and spray attachments.

Faucets come in two basic materials and a near-limitless number of styles. The materials are brass and plastic. The former is highly recommended, together with ceramic disks inside to control water flows.

Faucet styles vary in handle shape and form, height and accessories. A single-lever model makes life easier in the kitchen [and, some would argue, in bathrooms as well]. Mechanical options include pull-out faucets with sprayers and built-in or separate water filters. And water can be dispensed through fittings that will accommodate pots and pans of almost any shape and size.

Finish options include chrome plating, nickel plating, white enamel, brass, colored epoxy, platinum, porcelain, bronze, stainless steel, gold and silver.

In making your choices you'll want to consider:

- Do sinks and faucets complement one another?

- Do sinks come with enough tap holes to accommodate the faucets and accessories you've selected?

- Is faucet height sufficient to fill tall pots?

- Do faucets complement the kitchen décor?

- Will faucets you've selected 'stand up' to the level of wear you'll give them?

- Will faucet cleaning be quick and easy?

- If faucets are to be used by elderly or disabled individuals, will they be suitable for such use?

- Will you be able to manipulate the controls when your hands are wet or sticky?

Notes

Chapter 18
Flooring

The perfect kitchen floor is comfortable, non-slip, impervious to spills, easily cleaned, and environmentally friendly.

No such material exists!

In flooring, as in countertops, you're going to be faced with a broad range of options – none of them perfect.

The most cushioning is found in vinyl, linoleum [in sheet or tile forms], and carpet.

Easy cleaning and spill resistance are attributes of vinyl, laminate and linoleum although stone, wood and concrete can be made spill-resistant with sealers.

Slip-resistance is lowest in marble and wood.

Let's take a look at the options individually to help you sort them out.

Vinyl gives you that resilient "bounce-back" feeling and comes in several varieties. Color and pattern go all the way through inlaid vinyl but are printed on standard vinyl. No-wax, water-resistant coatings are applied to both. Vinyl comes in sheet and tile form and in a broad range of colors and patterns. It won't discolor when exposed to water, is easy to sweep and mop and resists scuffs and stains. Spills should be cleaned up quickly, however, in that stain resistant does not mean stain-proof. And the surface can be marred or scarred by dropped utensils, high heels, etc.

Laminate on fiberboard or particleboard can provide the look of hardwood or stone with easier maintenance and lower cost. The material is durable and traffic-resistant, cleans up easily and won't stain or fade. When it wears out, however, the entire floor must be replaced and laminate can chip and break up if water penetrates seams.

Stone – granite, marble and slate – is tough, durable, and can be installed over radiant heating systems. But it's cold, requires regular resealing to resist stains, can be slippery, and is susceptible to chipping. Light-colored grouts also can show stains. [Caution: natural colors vary. Approve slabs that will become your flooring before they're processed.]

Tile comes in several types: ceramic, made from pressed clay and covered with glaze or matte surface; porcelain mosaic, in which color goes all the way through; and quarry, an unglazed mix of shale and clay which also is colored throughout. Epoxy grouting is recommended for stain resistance. Tile comes in many sizes, patterns and colors. The glazed variety is stain-resistant and requires no special maintenance but may be slippery. Unglazed tile requires sealing and regular resealing. And all varieties of tile are hard on the feet.

Wood floors come in two varieties: finished on site and pre-finished. They usually are fabricated of oak or maple although pine occasionally is used. Where on-site finishing is used, planks, strips or parquet squares are installed before cabinets and finished with penetrating oil and wax. Most pre-finished flooring is polyurethane-coated and usually is installed after cabinets. Finished-on-site flooring is less than ideal in high-traffic areas where the risk of spills is high. Warping or buckling may occur should water seep into spaces between boards.

Linoleum, often confused with vinyl because both come in sheet form, has returned to popularity as an environmentally-friendly product. It's made from natural materials – felt or canvas coated with linseed oil, cork and resins – rather than the synthetics used in vinyl. Linoleum is smooth, elastic and comfortable. It resists oil and grease but can be damaged by standing water and comes in fewer colors and patterns than vinyl.

Concrete has come out of the basement! Multiple colors and finishes are available and the material absorbs heat, making it ideal for radiant heating systems. Concrete is as durable as stone and tile but requires sealing to prevent staining. The material's weight can be a problem other than on slab foundations and hard falls can be dangerous for children and the elderly.

Carpet is quieter and more comfortable than any other flooring. But common kitchen spills are difficult to clean up and major accidents [picture a pot of spaghetti] can be disastrous. A tight berber manufactured of olefin or another stain-resistant material is recommended if you must have carpet.

Notes

Notes

Chapter 19
Lighting

Lighting is more important in a kitchen than in any other room in the house with the possible exception of milady's bathroom [those of the male persuasion rarely deal with the imperceptible shadings in tone and color that render makeup acceptable or unacceptable to the female of the species].

Bathroom lighting can be supplemented with table lamps and lighted mirrors, however, while kitchen lighting fixtures are permanently attached and difficult [if not impossible] to relocate once installed. Kitchen lighting can be installed:

- In or on ceilings.

- Under cabinets.

- In cabinets.

Lighting unit also are categorized as to purpose: general, task or accent. Accent lighting, as in the case of in-cabinet illumination, is decorative. Task lighting is directed toward specific work or task areas – sinks, cooking surfaces, etc. General lighting [in or on the ceiling] is created to illuminate the room.

The bulk of lighting fixtures are fluorescent or incandescent although improving technology is leading to greater variety in bulbs and in quality of light. Two technical variables are worthy of attention in considering overall kitchen lighting plans: power consumption and heat generation. Both influence utility bills.

Ideally, the kitchen lighting scheme will provide ample illumination to meet the utilitarian needs of the user and lower-level lighting to make the area easily accessible but more dimly illuminated when meals are not in preparation. This goal can be achieved by installing multiple lighting circuits and/or by incorporating rheostats or dimmer switches.

88   Creating Your New Kitchen

[Note: while incandescent lighting is amenable to dimming, fluorescent tubes are either on or off. There is no middle ground.]

You'll want to consider a number of factors in making your choices:

- The appearance of the fixtures.

- How accurately the light renders colors.

- Whether multiple light sources of different types will be compatible.

- The quantity of light needed.

- Energy requirements specified by governmental agencies.

- Your budget.

Ceiling lighting usually is recessed [fixtures are in the ceiling rather than on the ceiling] and most often consists of fluorescent fixtures, incandescent "cans" or a combination of the two. Fluorescent fixtures are usually less expensive to install and operate. They often are criticized for their "commercial appearance" and, until recently, for the relative harshness of their light. Today's incandescent bulbs and fluorescent tubes are available in a broad range of models and types, each of them furnishing a different quality of light.

The commercial appearance is difficult to avoid but light quality can be made more acceptable by using "daylight" or "sunlight" rather than the more common blue-white fluorescent tubes.

In recent years, ceiling lighting in kitchens occasionally has been augmented with miniature halogen "track lights" —miniatures of the spotlights used in retail establishments, art galleries, and the like. Tracks must be attached to the ceiling rather than being recessed but most are available in white to blend into, rather than contrasting with, the ceiling.

Under-cabinet or concealed strip lighting has grown in popularity as advancing technology has permitted manufacturers to make fixtures smaller without sacrificing light output. Fixtures now can be installed that are all-but-invisible to any standing adult and that eliminate the dark shadows otherwise thrown on countertops by wall cabinets.

In-cabinet lighting has benefited from the same trend in combination with one other: the increasing use of glass-doored cabinets. This development has encouraged homeowners to display more and more decorative glassware and dishes – items once largely concealed by solid cabinet doors. The ability to turn cabinets into kitchen displays, in turn, led to in-cabinet lighting.

Lighting alternatives also can be examined in terms of types of fixtures to be used.

Ceiling strip lights provide the most light for the least money. The light emitted by fluorescent strips is rather harsh, however, even where modern, color-corrected tubes are used. Incandescent strips give a warmer, yellower light.

Pendant lights are increasingly popular, especially in kitchens of more modern design. Fixtures should be matched to the style of the room and should be positioned so that they don't glare in occupants' eyes. Simple designs that don't catch dirt and grease are most desirable.

Track-mounted spotlights provide considerable flexibility because they can be aimed at almost any work area. They create shadows, however, and will produce glare when reflected from shiny surfaces.

Recessed incandescent ceiling lights, or "down lights" as they're sometimes called, are neat and inconspicuous. Narrow and wide-beam bulbs are available and some fixtures permit bulbs to be aimed or angled.

Wall-mounted uplights can be used to "bounce" light off light-colored ceilings and help eliminate shadows. They are available with incandescent or halogen bulbs. While more expensive, the halogen fixtures generate much more light.

Kitchen lighting should be planned with one guideline in mind: beware of shadows and glare. Kitchens must be shadow and glare-free. That means fixtures must be positioned so that no one can stand between the fixture and the area being lighted.

Task lighting is best provided through concealed strip lights positioned beneath wall cabinets. Pendant lights positioned over counters also can be used, as can angled work lamps on shelves or counters.

Illumination also is needed at the sink and over the cooktop. Over-sink lighting is easily provided by a single down light fixture in the ceiling. Spotlight bulbs should be avoided, however, because they tend to produce glare.

Many range hoods incorporate light fixtures – some good and some bad. In better fixtures, bulbs or strip lights are enclosed to protect them from heat and grease splatters.

Notes

Chapter 20
Architectural Detail

What's architectural detail?

It's a material category that might also be called "everything else." It includes walls and ceilings, windows and doors, moldings and those one-of-a-kind items that you might want to incorporate into your new kitchen.

These are the "finishing touches" that make the kitchen distinctly yours; the "trimmings" that reflect your tastes and preferences.

Where do you begin? Logically, with the design and color schemes that predominate in the home and – especially – in the nearby rooms. You've already considered these elements in selecting cabinetry and countertops, of course, but that still leaves a great deal to be done.

The accents you introduce can be subtle, enhancing other design elements, or strong, becoming focal points in themselves. In either case, you'll want to approach the details with care, recognizing that these "little things" can make major differences in the appearance of your new kitchen. And in every case you'll want to keep in your primary objectives in mind.

The accents you deploy to make the kitchen most appealing to prospective homebuyers probably would be very different from those you'd select to complement your own furnishings and color scheme. Other than as to those one-of-a-kind items, such as the antique table you'd take with you when you move, every architectural detail is a necessity rather than an "extra."

As such, they deserve care in selection and installation to complement and enhance one another and the kitchen as a whole. You'll doubtless want to revisit your color and texture options before you begin. Reason: the choices you make will exercise a strong influence on the overall appearance of the room.

Color experts suggest using three colors in a room – one on about 60 percent of the area, a second on 30 percent, and a third on 10 percent. The impact of color on appearance is well-known:

- Space will appear to expand where you use cool, light or dull colors with minimum contrast.

- Space will appear to shrink under the impact of warm, dark or bright colors and high contrast.

- Ceilings lower when painted in warm colors and/or dark tones but are heightened in appearance with cool colors and light tints.

- Rooms appear shorter where colors are warm or dark and longer where contrast is limited and cool, light, or dull colors are used.

- And undesirable features can be hidden where their colors blend into surrounding colors.

Textures are equally important where considered in tactile and visual terms. Textures add contrast and interest. Other than as to tile and moldings, most kitchen materials are smooth. You'll find considerable variation in visual interest, however, when you examine laminate, solid surface, stone, wood, tile, concrete, stainless steel and vinyl or linoleum.

Notes

Chapter 21
Walls and Ceilings

At least nine "finishes" can be applied to walls and ceilings, which usually are made of drywall or gypsum board covered by one or more. They include:

- Paint
- Vinyl wall coverings or wallpaper
- Wood paneling
- Metal
- Plaster
- Exposed brick
- Concrete
- Ceramic tile
- Solid surface

Exposed beams or rafters – merely decorative as well as structural -- also can be used on ceilings.

These materials must be evaluated in light of the kitchen environment, which is relatively humid and often contains large amounts of airborne grease, smoke, and other elements that ultimately must be removed from all surfaces.

Paints are used far differently in today's households than once was the case. The color spectrum has exploded and the modern paint store can match any color or shade. More important, monotone applications are being replaced by "faux finishes" incorporating two or more paint colors applied in layers.

Painted surfaces thus can take on almost any appearance. They can look like marble or other varieties of stone; like coarse or fine fabrics; or – where murals are used – like any landscape or seascape.

In all cases, paint used in kitchens should be limited to durable alkyd-based or water-based latex varieties. The alkyd-based paints are most durable. Both varieties are available in a range of finishes, from dull to high gloss.

'**Wallpaper,**' for reasons specified above, should be limited to vinyl varieties because they are easier to clean. Fortunately, this is not a limiting factor. Vinyl wall coverings today range from murals [usually far less expensive than the painted variety] to almost any conceivable pattern and color.

Wood can be used, but must be applied with care to prevent maintenance problems. The products involved range from paneling to raw planks. Pre-finished [and sealed] paneling, available in most woods and finishes, can be installed with relative ease. Finished-in-place paneling or planks also can be used but must be handled carefully.

Wood is porous by nature. It can absorb moisture and other airborne materials unless protected by polyurethane finishes or similarly efficient sealants.

Metal wall coverings – usually in the form of tiles – do not share wood's absorbency. Stainless steel sheets or tiles often are used in residential as well as commercial kitchens – especially those with "modern" designs. Almost any other metal can be similarly applied. Users must be sensitive, however, to potential for discoloration.

Brick and concrete also are creeping into contemporary kitchens, usually to surround a range or pizza oven and add "authenticity." Unfortunately, these materials share the absorbency problem of wood. They must be sealed at the outset and periodically resealed to protect against grease, smoke, and other elements that can cause discoloration.

Ceramic tile is available in a range of types, styles and finishes. Tile is often used in backsplashes and – where surfaces are hard [shiny] – is not difficult to clean. Porous tile can absorb splashes and splatters, however, as can the grout used between tiles. The latter problem can be minimized by using epoxy grout, which is available in almost any color a homeowner might want.

Solid surface material [the same product used in countertops and integral sinks] is among the best of materials for backsplash panels. The finish is impervious to grease and food stains and the material can be had in almost any color. [Suggestion: if you've used solid surface countertops with contrasting edges or integral sinks you might consider using the edge or sink color in the backsplash panels.]

Notes

Notes

Chapter 22
Windows and Doors

A rose is a rose is a rose, a poet wrote. Many think of windows in the same way: they're all about the same.

Wrong!

Today they come many styles and designs, and with a number of noteworthy technical options. Styles and designs:

- Double hung [the traditional window], which slide vertically or horizontally.

- Casement, which are crank-operated and swing horizontally outward.

- Rotary, which move on a central pivot.

- Greenhouse, which are the vertical-swinging equivalent of casements.

- Clerestory, placed in the upper portions of walls.

- Cathedral, arched windows that usually do not open.

- Bay, set in bays constructed in walls – often in dinettes.

- Sliding, the horizontal equivalent of double hung.

And don't forget skylights!

One way or another, you'll want considerable light in your kitchen. Some can come from an adjacent dinette or sunroom but the National Kitchen and Bath Association recommends that you nevertheless allocate at least 10 percent of your kitchen floor space [in square feet] to windows.

Today's more significant differences in windows involve the ways in which they're constructed. Consumers can choose between single and double-pane varieties, between conventional and coated glass, between windows with Venetian blinds built in and windows without.

All of these are factors in energy conservation. Two panes of glass conduct less heat and cold. The coatings filter out ultraviolet and infrared light. Internal blinds reduce conductivity -- and don't need cleaning.

Skylights are useful where windows are shaded and kitchens are darker than desired but they're only marginally useful as energy-saving devices. Their ability to admit light declines as the sun goes down – the same time that most start reaching for light switches.

Windows and doors should be selected to complement exterior decors and the design of the home in its' entirety. Kitchen door materials include wood, fiberglass, steel and glass [where the homemaker wants to use sliding French doors onto a patio or deck]. Transoms and/or sidelights can be used to admit more light where space for traditional windows is limited.

Notes

Chapter 23
Molding and Trim

Moldings are highly versatile devices that can be used to create a more polished finish in a room, to decorate cabinets or to ease transitions from one wall material to another – for example, between paneling and plaster or between brick and plaster.

They can be costly or economically manufactured from hardwoods in the first instance or from rigid, vinyl-coated foam in the second.

You'll find moldings and trim to be of little value in minimal, uncluttered contemporary kitchens but of significant help in executing more traditional themes such as French country or similarly complex designs.

Hand-carved crown moldings, panels and corbels are quite at home in kitchens of the latter sort. Moldings can be stacked to further strengthen visual impact and rope, dentil fluting and other elaborate designs can contribute to the overall impact.

Notes

Notes

Chapter 24
One-of-a-Kind Items

An antique desk integrated into the kitchen design.

An old dresser incorporated into an island.

A wrought iron gate transformed to become an overhead rack for pots and pans.

These are exemplary of the one-of-kind items homeowners are incorporating into their kitchens.

The list need not be restricted to items of furniture. An old clock would prove equally eye-catching. So would an antique washtub or washing machine. The flea markets and antique shops are awash with antiquities that can add focal points to kitchen designs.

All you need do is find them, or create them from among your own attic's treasurers or those of your family.

Notes

Notes

Section V
The Construction Process

You've made all the decisions. The contracts have been signed. Now you can relax while the work gets done.

Wrong again!

Now that you've made all the necessary choices, you want action! Realistically, you're looking for instant gratification [aren't we all]. But you're going to experience more frustration during construction than you encountered in making all those difficult choices.

Unless you're dealing with a new home rather than a renovation, you'd best plan on a month of construction. It might be less. But it also could require a few more days to do everything you've decided you want done.

Notes

Notes

Chapter 25
Scheduling

You're going to find that decisions made in haste often are, indeed, repented at leisure. For example, if you decided to add an island – complete with cook top, sink and refrigerator – where none previously existed, you've added considerable time and inconvenience to the project.

Consider what has to be done in order to install the island. You'll need pipes, power lines and [unless other provisions have been made for ventilation] a conduit for air and vapor drawn off by a downdraft system. These can be installed with relative ease if there's a crawl space or basement beneath the existing kitchen. Otherwise, a jackhammer probably will have to be used to cut channels into the existing concrete floor. Then conduits will have to be installed and concrete poured over them before any *real* installation work can begin on the new kitchen.

Structural changes such as those described above, or those involved in moving an existing wall, can add considerably to project time requirements. If the wall is not load-bearing, and if it contains no ductwork or power lines that have to be relocated, it probably can be moved in a day [plus whatever time is necessary to re-plaster and paint. Where electrical, plumbing or heating lines are involved, time factors compound.

The problem is one of coordination. Your contractor will have to schedule carpenters, plasterers [or sheet rock installers], plumbers, electricians, heating technicians and others. If each arrives and completes his work on time, the project proceeds smoothly. But that's rarely the case for several reasons.

> First, technicians can't be held to specific appointment times, even if their work will require only a matter of minutes or a few hours. The best you can expect is a promise – which may or may not be kept – to arrive during a morning or afternoon.

106   Creating Your New Kitchen

Your general contractor probably will allow a day – perhaps two – for each craftsman.

Second, moving a wall is a two-step process – removing the old and installing the new. This mean that each craftsman usually has to make at least two visits – one to tear out and the other to install.

Third, and most importantly, any delay on the part of one craftsman will require rescheduling all those who follow.

You're paying your contractor to coordinate subcontractors' schedules, of course, but he's more dependent on them than they are on him – unless you're wise enough to select a larger renovation contractor whose work is prized by sub-contractors. Even then, you can't expect perfection. Let's look at the sequence of events that must take place.

First are the structural changes such as moving walls, removing soffits or drop-downs [they're rarely used any more], adding skylights or bay windows, etc. Changes such as these must be completed before any installation work can begin. As indicated earlier, structural changes usually are accomplished through a two-step process: tearing out the old and installing the new.

Second is assembling necessary materials. Cabinets, appliances, flooring, wall coverings and other components can require weeks – or months – for delivery. Custom cabinets, for example, typically must be ordered three to four months in advance. Semi-custom units require two to 2 ½ months. Stock cabinetry may be available in a matter of days but you'd best count on a month. You'll have to provide space to store all these materials until they're needed, which also will complicate your life in one way or another.

Third, any remaining old cabinetry, appliances and other components of the existing kitchen must be removed. That process will require at least one day; perhaps two.

Fourth come mechanical changes: plumbing, electrical, heating/air conditioning. [These consist of new lines and rerouting of old lines other than as may be needed in the course of structural changes.] At least two to three days will be required but you'll be safest allowing a day for each trade or craft.

Fifth, counter tops must be installed. The installation process seldom requires more than a day but the tops must be ordered a month or more in advance depending on materials involved.

Sixth are new wall finishes – paint, wallpaper and the like. Numbers of finishes and numbers of crafts involved govern time requirements. Allow at least two days.

Seventh [after walls have been completed] is flooring. Installation time depends on the materials you've selected. Linoleum and parquet go down quickly. Concrete, finished-in-place wood and other material can require considerably more time.

With walls and floor complete the space is ready for installation of:

- Cabinetry, which will take two to 10 working days.

- Appliances, which can be installed in a day or two.

- Lighting, which usually can be completed in two days.

- Back splashes, at least two days.

- Sinks, at least one day.

- Cook top(s), at least one day.

Keep in mind when developing your installation time estimates that "installation" can be a two-step process consisting [in the case of appliances, for example] of placement and installation. A deliveryman can put a garbage disposal unit in place but it takes a plumber [and, perhaps, an electrician] to hook up the unit after it's installed.

Notes

Chapter 26
Potential Installation Problems

Remember "the best laid plans of mice and men ...?"

How about "anything that can go wrong will go wrong?"

And then there's "hope for the best but plan for the worst."

There's more wisdom than poetry in all these admonitions. Your renovation project and – and often will – be plagued by any number of problems. Among them:

- Late arrivals on the part of workers, materials or both.

- In-transit or factory damage to components ranging from cabinetry to appliances to floor and wall coverings.

- Parts missing.

- Incomplete shipments.

- Unanticipated hidden damage [termites, dry rot, carpenter ants, etc.] that must be repaired before work can proceed.

- Water damage in walls due to old plumbing leaks.

- Structural problems [misaligned walls; sagging floors] that have to be remedied before work can continue.

- Rotting windows, frames, sills, etc.

- Construction damage in adjacent rooms or spaces.

- Asbestos removal in older buildings.

You'll have no choice but to roll with the punches. These are elements no contractor can anticipate that always result in added costs and construction delays.

Your primary task is going to be to survive the delays, which means minimizing the impact of the construction, maintaining some semblance of household stability, and preserving functional relationships with contractor, vendors and workers as well as inconvenienced family members.

Notes

Chapter 27
Survival

Completing a kitchen renovation with one's nerves intact requires careful planning, especially in three areas: dust control, breakage control and preparation.

The three are necessarily linked together unless you can isolate the work area from the remainder of the home. That goal can be accomplished, but at a rather high price: you'll have to abandon the kitchen and any other areas involved "for the duration."

Total isolation will permit you to minimize the volume of dust that reaches other parts of the house. Remember the word "minimize." Dust can't be kept out. But it can be controlled.

You'll want to obtain [or have your contractor provide] a large roll of plastic sheeting and several rolls of masking tape. Use them to seal doorways and passageways between the work area and the other parts of the house. Use the same materials to cover bookcases, furniture and electronic equipment [computers are especially vulnerable to dust and dirt].

You may want to consider using a blower of some sort to increase the air pressure on "your side" of these barriers while work is in progress. If pressure is higher in work areas, leakage into living areas will bring dust with airflows.

If possible [you'll have to consult your heating/air conditioning company on this one] shut down air returns from work areas to your heating/air conditioning units. At minimum, install high efficiency filters to trap as much dust as possible and prevent it's being "broadcast" throughout the building by heating or air conditioning blowers.

The dust problem will be pervasive. The protection issue is more easily managed. You'll want to move wall hangings [pictures, mirrors, etc.], and other items in rooms adjacent to the construction area away from joint walls. Vibration from construction activities [such as jackhammering concrete] otherwise may produce breakage.

Your final preparation for the start of construction should involve survival during the temporary absence of the kitchen and its' contents. You'll want to consider:

- Establishing a "mini-cooking-center" consisting of a microwave oven and/or hot plate, refrigerator and coffee pot. You'll also need disposable "cutlery" and dishes, garbage and trash bags, and foods.

- Preparing to do without water for hours or days while plumbing changes are made and new kitchen fixtures are installed. You'll want to arrange to do dishes elsewhere, or stock up on disposables.

- Collecting restaurants' promotional coupons in anticipation of the "absent" kitchen for the weeks involved.

Notes

Chapter 28
Communication

Your contractor will want to be your friend when the new kitchen is complete – if only because he'll want you to call on him again. He'll do everything he can to avoid problems during construction, and to make certain you know what's going on at all times.

But communication is a two-way street. The objective is shared understanding. You'll want to know in advance ...

- Whether tearing out the old kitchen will begin before everything needed for the new is on hand.

- Who [you or the contractor] will store materials until work begins.

- How the contractor, his sub-contractors, and their personnel will access the premises [ideally, you'll be able to provide a separate entrance – a back door or side door].

- That all necessary permits have been obtained from municipal and/or county building or construction departments.

- That the freight elevator will be available as needed if you live in an apartment.

- That you have a complete list of office and cellular telephone numbers as well as beeper numbers for all contractor and subcontractor personnel.

And you'll want to keep your contractor aware of any questions or issues that arise in the course of the work.

Notes

Chapter 29
Helpful Tips

- A preparation area between cooktop and refrigerator saves time and effort.

- Place the refrigerator away from the main activity at the end of a run of cabinets so it can be used without interfering with the cook.

- Minimize plumbing and ventilation runs to keep costs down.

- Mix cabinet heights and combine solid and glass door fronts to avoid visual monotony.

- Put halogen downlights in the base of wall cabinets to light collectibles.

- Use fluorescent strip lights under cabinets to illuminate food preparation areas and eliminate shadows.

- Use adjustable shelves for maximum efficiency in use of wall cabinet space.

- Use wall space between countertop and cabinets for shallow drawers or shelving.

- Plan drawers in multiple widths and depths, and equip with dividers for best use of drawer space.

- Use wine racks only for wines served at room temperature and stored for short periods. Wine deteriorates rapidly in changing kitchen temperatures.

- Use shallow drawers to store kitchen utensils and linens.

- Narrow pull-out cabinets are useful for tall bottles and herb or spice containers.

- Use countertop, backsplash and flooring colors to complement rather than blend into cabinetry.

- Position the refrigerator away from heat sources and close to eating and relaxing areas for easy access.

- Don't place your cooktop in a corner where space is restricted. Convenience requires workspace on both sides.

- A floor-to-ceiling pullout pantry will add considerable storage space.

- Consider placing the refrigerator near the door so groceries can be quickly unloaded without disturbing others in the kitchen.

- A projecting counter can be doubly useful as a combination countertop-breakfast bar.

- Use a bi-fold or pocket doors to conserve space in small kitchens.

- Compact appliances – narrower than standard – can save space in small kitchens.

- Lowering one section of countertop creates space ideal for rolling pastry, kneading dough or chopping vegetables – and adds to visual variety as well.

- Where counter space is scarce, consider recessing a sink into the countertop and doing without a drain board.

- Create a visual link between kitchen and adjacent living area with a coordinated color scheme.

- Islands usually require electrical outlets and may need plumbing and gas lines as well.

Creating Your New Kitchen 117

- Cooking areas must be well-ventilated to keep odors, grease and steam from drifting into adjacent living areas.

- Portable islands in wood or stainless steel add flexibility and workspace to the kitchen.

- Storage for china, flatware and glasses should be organized so the table can be set without crossing other activity areas.

- Keep sharp knives in shallow drawers with narrow compartments. They'll be easier to locate and blades will stay sharper than if they were allowed to knock against one another.

- Fresh fruits and vegetables are best stored in chiller drawers beneath food preparation areas rather than refrigerator bins.

- A small secondary sink and chopping area will help keep children and guests away from ovens and range.

- How easy or difficult will it be for adjacent cabinet and/or appliance doors to be opened at the same time? Check on it, and make adjustments where necessary.

- Position your sink so that the user will face into the room to talk with guests or watch television.

- Pullout pantry units that make every item accessible always outperform the traditional closet or pantry.

- Position refrigerator and freezer adjacent to a surface that can handle heavy bags while content is unpacked and stored.

- Select your refrigerator and freezer with front vents so they'll fit flush to walls and minimize accumulation of dust.

- Be certain that shelves can be adjusted to accommodate large boxes and tall bottles as well as cans and jars.

- Provide a well-ventilated drawer or cabinet for cookies, cakes, pastries and other food best stored at room temperature.

- Often-underused overhead space can help meet storage needs if equipped with a hanging rack for pans and utensils or shelves for seasonings.

- Use sturdy drawers with shallow sides to create easy-access storage for heavy pots and pans.

- Adjustable metal shelving, removable for cleaning in the dishwasher, is an excellent choice for solid-door cabinets.

- Tile, stone and similar materials that can be scrubbed clean are preferred for backsplashes.

- A pullout spray nozzle provides added cleaning power at the sink.

- A removable cutting board lets a sink do double duty as a temporary work surface for slicing or chopping.

- The perfect ventilation system can cope with the volume of steam the kitchen generates without making conversation difficult.

- Task lights beneath ventilation hoods let cooks see into pots and pans.

- Adjustable plate racks near cooking surfaces warm plates and make them ready for use.

- Wrap and foil are most easily accessed when placed in wall-mounted dispensers.

- Sinks should be close enough to cooktops to permit heavy pans to be easily moved from one to the other.

Creating Your New Kitchen 119

- Check oven capacities before making selections. Insulation and self-cleaning equipment can reduce interior dimensions.

- Digital temperature displays and "ready" lights on ovens make for easier use.

- Select items of kitchen equipment individually on their merits. They need not match and can be placed behind cabinet fronts if necessary.

- Make certain appliances provide sufficient capacity for your needs.

- Inquire about the availability of service for the appliances you prefer to avoid unacceptable waiting times when help is needed.

- Consider adding a warming drawer to extend the capabilities of your oven.

- Demand a cooktop with a smooth, crevice-free surround to minimize clean-up problems.

- Easily-cleaned wire mesh filters are preferable in ventilating hoods.

- Cooktop elements in varying sizes permit users to select just the right pan for the job and conserve energy.

- Examine the way refrigerator doors open and make certain you allow enough space for them to be opened fully.

- Glass or grid shelving in refrigerators helps to illuminate interiors.

- Round sinks may be attractive but have less capacity than square versions.

- Pans and glassware that require hand washing are best handled with a bowl-and-a-half sink configuration.

- An awkward corner can be conquered with a corner sink – two bowls set at a 90 degree angle.

- Drain boards' tendency to consume valuable space can be avoided by using those can be stored when not in use.

- Faucets should swivel easily to fill either bowl in a two-bowl sink. A high arc or swan neck design creates maximum flexibility.

- Dishwashers equipped with two spray arms do a superior job.

- Make certain your new dishwasher has an anti-flood sensor that shuts off water flows when a leak is detected.

- Concealed dishwasher controls [in the top edge of the door] prevent their use by small children.

- A dishwasher with a stainless steel interior can be expected to last for 20 years.

- Front-loading washing machines require less water and detergent.

- Top-loading washing machines can be opened while operating to add a forgotten item.

- Self-leveling or adjustable feet are essential in washing machines to compensate for any irregularities in the floor.

- Self-balancing washing machine tubs prevent imbalances from developing while loads are being washing.

- Consider front-loading, under-counter washer/dryer combinations where space is at a premium.

Creating Your New Kitchen   121

- Compartmented drawers or cabinets make recycling easier.

- A waste hole in a countertop leading to a lined drawer below makes life easier for those who use high volumes of vegetables and fresh fruit.

- Waste disposal units are not recommended where septic tanks are in use.

- Limit composting waste to vegetable matter. Bread, meat, and fish smell and attract files and rodents.

- Laminated surfaces resist abrasion but can be damaged by sharp objects and hot pans.

- Terra-cotta floor tiles are porous and must be sealed to prevent staining.

- Wood flooring is easy to maintain but can be dented if heavy items or dropped and may warp in the presence of heat and/or moisture.

- Custom-formulated kitchen paints resist moisture, grease and mildew.

- Using chopping blocks will prolong the life of countertops.

- Cabinets that can survive rough treatment are preferred in households with small children.

- Pale surfaces require more cleaning.

- Heavily textured surfaces should be avoided in food preparation and cooking areas in that crevices hold dirt and grease.

- Careful maintenance is required to prevent staining of wood surfaces by water, juice and oil.

- Textured surfaces appear shinier and darker under artificial lighting.

- Natural brick walls provide pattern and texture but require water-repellant sealing.

- Mosaic tiles are provided on backing sheets, permitting individual sections or tiles to be easily removed and replaced.

- Glass or clear plastic back splashes are easily cleaned and let wall color show through.

- Color matching is critical where laminated surfaces are intended to match cabinetry.

- Use waterproof grouting to set kitchen tiles. It's easier to clean and outlasts standard cement mixes.

- Halogen track lighting creates visual interest over large expanses of ceiling or wall.

- Contemporary rise-and-fall pendant light fixtures adapt well to dining areas.

- Fluorescent tubes should be shielded to protect eyes against their harsh, glaring light.

- Limestone tiles resist water, heat and household chemicals after careful sealing.

- Rubber stud flooring is easy to install and tough enough for public buildings.

- Terra cotta flooring is hardwearing and comfortable to walk on without shoes.

- Glazed ceramic tile used in floors will be slippery unless limited to textured varieties.

- Slate floors are hard and cold underfoot but will last forever.

- Lacquered wood cabinet tops complement most cabinetry but are prone to marring.

- Granite is the most durable of natural materials in countertops.

- Stone counters can be routed to help drainage, eliminating the need for a sink draining board.

- Stainless steel is the ideal countertop material in sink and cooktop areas.

- Mix and match countertops to demands of specific work areas.

- Counters with rounded, postformed or bullnose edges minimize injury potential.

- Tile counters perform well in cooking areas but grout can collect dirt and may be hard to clean.

- Multiple counter levels make activities such as baking convenient and comfortable.

- Backsplash and countertops should be planned concurrently so that materials complement one another.

- Polyester cabinet finishes are hard-wearing and easily cleaned but abrasives will dull their finishes.

- Bright metal knobs and trim make eye-catching cabinet features.

- Lacquer finishes provide a tough, protective alternative to costly polyesters.

- Consistency in grain and color are vital in using wood finishes over large areas in that differences are obvious.

- Glass-doored cabinets create a feeling of spaciousness in a small kitchen.

- Combining cabinet finishes, such as laminate panels with natural wood, prevent monotony in large expanses of cabinets.

- Polishing with the grain and regular buffing help maintain the appearance of solid wood cabinets.

- Consider natural stone floors and white walls with natural wood cabinet finishes.

- Distressed finishes add years of care and wear to cabinetry.

- Use limed finishes for a pale, grainy look that's lighter and more adaptable than heavy stains.

- Use furnishings that are easily removed for cleaning.

- Shiny finishes reflect light and can cause glare while matte finishes create a softer look by absorbing and diffusing light.

- Remove old wall covering before installing new rather than risk having grease work its way through the layers.

- Cooktop backsplashes must resist steam, heat, grease and splashes.

Chapter 30
Record-keeping

Changes are inevitable in any major construction project, and creating a new kitchen falls within that category in terms of complexity as well as size. You're going to encounter problems. Some may be economic. Others will deal with suppliers. Some of the things you want are going to be too expensive. Items you've selected will have been discontinued or won't be available for delivery as needed.

Handling such problems can be difficult unless you've prepared for contingencies and kept adequate records. Contingencies are easily handled when you've prepared a "fall-back position" for each decision. "If we can't get A, we'll use B."

This sort of preparation is easy when you plan accordingly "from day one." That's why we've prepared the following charts for your convenience. If you'll take time to use them – to record complete information concerning your first choices and alternatives in every category – you'll be ready to handle the changes that inevitably have to be made in creating your new kitchen.

Range	Preferred	Alternate
Manufacturer		
Model No.		
Price		
Fuel [electric/gas]		
Btu's		
Size		
Color		
Source		
Availability		
Cooktop	**Preferred**	**Alternate**
Manufacturer		
Model No.		
Price		
Fuel [electric/gas]		

Btu's		
Size		
Color		
Source		
Availability		

Oven	**Preferred**	**Alternate**
Manufacturer		
Model No.		
Price		
Fuel [electric/gas]		
[ ] Single [ ] Double		
Size		
Color		
Source		
Availability		

Cabinetry	**Preferred**	**Alternate**
Manufacturer		
Style No.		
Price		
Material		
Finish		
Door style		
No. glass-front doors		
No. base cabinets		
No. wall cabinets		
Source		
Availability		

Flooring	Preferred	Alternate
Manufacturer		
Style No.		
Price		
Square footage		
Color		
Material		
Source		
Availability		

Countertop	Preferred	Alternate
Manufacturer		
Style No.		
Price		
Linear footage		
Material		
Edge treatment		
Backsplash		
Source		
Availability		

Hood	Preferred	Alternate
Manufacturer		
Model No.		
Price		
Size		
Color		
Air flow [CFM]		
Source		
Availability		

128   *Creating Your New Kitchen*

Refrigerator	Preferred	Alternate
Manufacturer		
Model No.		
Price		
Style		
Size		
Color		
Decorative panel		
Source		
Availability		

Dishwasher	Preferred	Alternate
Manufacturer		
Model No.		
Price		
Size		
Color		
Decorative panel		
Source		
Availability		

Primary sink	Preferred	Alternate
Manufacturer		
Model No.		
Price		
Number of bowls		
Material		
Size		
Source		
Availability		

Second sink	Preferred	Alternate
Manufacturer		
Model No.		
Price		
Number of bowls		
Material		
Size		
Source		
Availability		

Faucet	Preferred	Alternate
Manufacturer		
Model No.		
Price		
Type of handle		
Pull-out		
Finish		
Number of holes		
Source		
Availability		

Notes